"Y'all, Julia Fowler just dills [...] y. If [...] your [...] an a [...] and [...] our language and customs. You might even time warp back to the nights your Mama made you sleep in sponge rollers or the first time you went cow tippin'. You might even taste the butter on your Mee Maw's homemade biscuits. Julia Fowler is to Southern comedy what white vinegar is to collard greens—absolutely necessary!"

♥ *Laura Bell Bundy*

SINGER AND SONGWRITER; TELEVISION, FILM, AND TONY-NOMINATED BROADWAY ACTRESS

JULIA FOWLER

GIBBS SMITH
TO ENRICH AND INSPIRE HUMANKIND

This book is dedicated to my Mama and Daddy, who are the finest Southerners I know; and to my darlin' Sam, for embracing all my Southern eccentricities.

19 20 21   5 4

Text © 2018 Julia Fowler

Published by
Gibbs Smith
P.O. Box 667
Layton, Utah 84041

1.800.835.4993 orders
www.gibbs-smith.com

Designed by Mina Bach

Printed and bound in China

Gibbs Smith books are printed on either recycled, 100% post-consumer waste, FSC-certified papers or on paper produced from sustainable PEFC-certified forest/controlled wood source.
Learn more at www.pefc.org.

Library of Congress Cataloging-in-Publication Data
Names: Fowler, Julia, 1971- author.
Title: Talk Southern to me : stories & sayings to accent your life /
Julia Fowler.
Description: First edition. | Layton, Utah : Gibbs Smith, 2017.
Identifiers: LCCN 2017032647
Subjects: LCSH: American wit and humor--Southern States. | Southern
States--Humor. | Southern States--Quotations, maxims, etc.
Classification: LCC PN6231.S64 F69 2017 | DDC 818/.602--dc23
LC record available at https://lccn.loc.gov/2017032647

ISBN: 978-1-4236-4896-3

Table of Contents

Introduction

The minute I open my mouth outside of the Deep South I'm asked the same question, "Are you from Texas?" So let me set the record straight. *Yes*, I have a big fat Southern accent that I wear as proudly as my granny's pearls, but I'm not from Texas. I was born and raised in the little town of Gaffney, South Carolina. Although my people are humble country folks who weren't rich, they gave me the richest foundation a gal could ever ask for—a Southern upbringing.

My childhood was saturated with Jesus and fried okra, lightning bugs and flip flops, yes ma'ams and no sirs, casseroles and cheese balls, taffeta and pom-poms, fishing and tubing, sponge rollers and hair spray, thank-you notes and social rules, pageants and tiaras, honeysuckle and honeybees, creeks and crawdads, moon pies and hayrides, pickup trucks and football games, magnolia trees and broken arms, sweet tea and skeeters, Myrtle Beach and Mason jars, and umpteen lessons. Lord the lessons . . . clogging, tap, jazz, ballet, piano, singing, baton, modeling, banjo, Irish step dancing, macramé, sign language, and endless hours of practicing my cursive writing. Thank you, Mama—I'm pretty darn proud of my handwriting, although admittedly, I've got no clue how to say that in sign language.

All those lessons led me down a path of lunacy called show business, where I found myself forced to live in two cities that were the polar opposite of the South—New York and Los Angeles. I have been blessed to work in TV, film, and on Broadway, and throughout, I've been constantly harassed about my Southern accent and grammar. When I would say things like, "Sugarbritches, unlatch that doomafloochie and raise that window down," city slickers would just stare at me like I was nuttier than a fruitcake.

Desperately missing the South and tired of being misunderstood, I decided to release my frustration through comedy. I gathered some my best friends who are hilarious Southern women and made a video that celebrated the *Sh%t Southern Women Say* and the humorous ways we say it. I had no idea if anybody would even watch my first video. But, my stars in heaven, the thing went viral and my YouTube Southern Women Channel was born.

My stars in heaven, the thing went viral . . .

Millions of views and many videos later, I have found a huge Internet community of folks who, like me, are proud as punch of their Southern heritage and parlance. There's just nothing like a good Southernism. While one could say, "Loretta had a bad face-lift," a Southerner says, "Loretta's had her face pulled tighter than a gnat's ass!" While one could say, "I'm very busy," a Southerner says, "Hun, I'm busier than a two-dollar hooker on nickel night." And while one could say, "That is useless," a Southerner says, "That's as useless as tits on a bull." No matter the situation, Southern folks always have an 'ism to fit the occasion.

♥ This book is a love letter to the South. As you read, I hope the stories, slang, and sayings will elicit memories of all the colorful, rib-tickling Southerners who have left an imprint on your life. Ultimately, it is Southerners who are responsible for keeping Southern traditions and phraseology alive. And if you're not from the South, bless your heart, pay attention 'cause there's a ton of wisdom to be found in these heartfelt, humorous expressions. Mama always said, "Sugar, your strength lies in your uniqueness," and she was right. Southerners speak their own unique version of the English language. It's a linguistic art. And it's gooder than grits, y'all.

XOXO
Julia Fowler

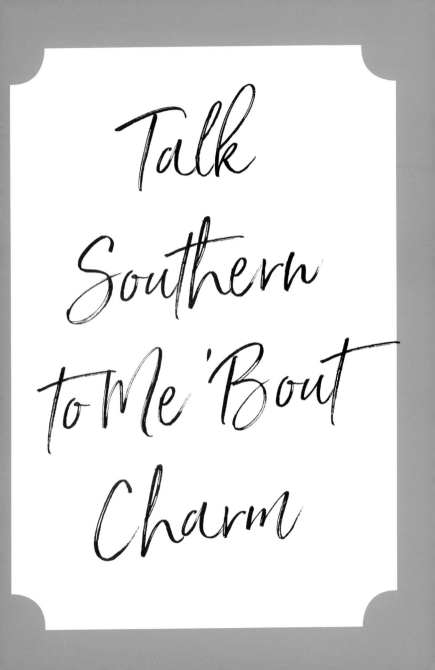

Talk Southern to Me 'Bout Charm

Charm

"Don't cost a nickel to be polite."

Southern hospitality is as indigenous to the South as magnolia trees. Having proper manners and displaying social grace in everyday actions is simply a way of life. It's an institution. And if you fail to follow these traditions, then your Southern family is liable to throw you in a mental institution. There are rules: you don't show up empty-handed to a dinner party even if you recently had both your hands amputated; if an elderly person is standing, then your younger butt better not be occupying a seat; and you never take store-bought food to a funeral reception even if your archenemy died. Southerners pass these kinds of rules down to the next generation so that they understand they are part of something bigger than themselves. The distinct Southern culture that has long defined the South would be extinct if older generations of Southerners weren't working harder than a one-eyed cat watching two mouse holes to preserve it.

In the South, good breeding is your legacy. And good breeding has nothing to do with money or education. I was raised by a blue-collar family who taught me that it "don't cost a nickel to be polite." Mastering the South's etiquette code and developing a sense of pride through social graces is considered more important than academics or wealth. Good manners teach you respect and self-discipline. Social graces give you composed confidence. When you combine these essential ingredients, you get the most delectable Southern dish of all: Southern charm.

Southern charm is the art of making everyone around you feel at ease. But Southern charm doesn't come naturally, y'all. No, no, no! You can't make others feel at ease unless you yourself have enough poise to feel at ease in a myriad of social and professional situations. So Southerners must start training early in life to develop the very charm that is the signature of the South. I graduated Magna Cum Laude from the University of South Carolina, but I assure you, many more grueling hours of effort were required pursuing my PhD in Southern charm. In order to acquire this degree, one must master four fundamental subjects: Politeness, Kindness, Table Manners, and Social Graces.

Politeness

Before I was even potty trained, my Southern family began training me to address my elders as "ma'am" and "sir" and to end sentences with "please" and "thank you." I was endlessly corrected and conditioned like a lab rat until, eventually, muscle memory kicked in and it became an ingrained habit. It's such second nature now that I have actually caught myself responding "yes ma'am" to an automated phone system. Southern boys are shaped into Southern gentlemen by this same method. But in addition to learning phrases like "ma'am" and "sir," Southern boys must also be schooled on Southern chivalry, such as opening doors and pulling out chairs, until it becomes cemented in their brains that all women should be treated as politely as they treat their Mamas.

Southern politeness also requires that you learn to write Pulitzer Prize–winning thank-you notes. My penmanship is exquisite because Mama drilled me on it like Archie Manning drilled Eli and Peyton on football. Seems downright unfair I can't get a multimillion-dollar

Emailing a thank-you note is the kiss of death ...

contract writing cursive. In any case, good handwriting is crucial because proper thank-you notes must be handwritten with a pen on decent card stock, preferably monogrammed, and the wording must be specific and thoughtful. And, most importantly, thank-you notes must be written and mailed in a timely fashion. Emailing a thank-you note is the kiss of death and will get you thrown out of the Junior League faster than a cat can lick its butt.

Southern politeness also demands that you greet everyone you encounter, friend or stranger, with a smile and a "Heeeeey, how are youuuuuuu?" And forgetting to wave when you drive by your neighbors or someone else you know is a cardinal sin. Even if your engine is on fire and your dog is biting your baby's ear off in the back seat, you must not forget this. Waving is of utmost impor-tance while driving. We call this the Southern "throw up." If you throw up one finger it means "Hey!" If you throw up two fingers it means "How y'all doing?" If you throw up your whole hand it means "How's your Mama and 'nem?" Throwing up nothing means "I'm a jackass."

KINDNESS

To secure a degree in Southern charm it's not enough to be polite; you must also become profi-cient in kindness. Kindness requires that you train yourself to constantly think of others. You must remember birthdays, anniversaries, and gradua-tions; acknowledge job promotions; and welcome new neighbors. This should be done with homemade cookies or cakes, homegrown vegetables or flowers from your garden, or thoughtfully selected note cards. Never send an Edible Arrangement—this screams tacky. You must also host and/or attend a gazillion baby and bridal showers and watch patiently as the gifts are opened in an elaborate display. And Southerners are competitive with their kindness, so one must go the extra mile to have gifts personalized with monograms, dig up a family heirloom, or at the very least spend half a year crocheting booties, needlepointing a pillow, or making a quilt the baby or the groom is certain to puke on within weeks.

Kindness also demands you acknowledge and engage in polite conversation with people in all walks of life: cashiers, plumbers, parking attendants, waiters, exterminators, secretaries, janitors, bail bondsmen. Southerners can learn a bank teller's entire life history while making a deposit. This is time consuming and contributes to the slow pace of the South, but Southern charm stipulates you embrace this turtle pace.

And no matter what, you must make time for the elderly. Southerners are extremely respectful of the elderly and go out of their way to extend kindness to them. I spent a substantial amount of my childhood performing in nursing homes. I did little shows featuring monologues, dance routines, piano playing—whatever my Mama deemed acceptable nursing home entertainment. Mama rehearsed me as if I was prepping to perform at Radio City Music Hall, and she didn't care how much time it took. Mama's kind heart was on a mission to bring joy to the residents of the nursing homes. She taught me that this was the char-itable thing to do even though the residents often slept and drooled through my mesmerizing clogging rendition of "Wabash Cannonball."

Kindness also dictates that you remember folks in their time of loss or despair. In the South, the appropriate response to every tragedy is a casserole. You must become a master chef of casseroles and you should develop an outstanding reputation for one variety that is your "signature casserole." I know women who make sure to keep a casserole frozen in their deep freezer so they are prepared when tragedy strikes. This is called a "disasterole." Doesn't matter if the disaster involves death, disease, or destruction—the Southern remedy is an avalanche of casseroles.

Table Manners

One of the primary reasons Southerners value both the cotillion and debutante traditions is because proper table manners are taught and they are key to evoking Southern charm. Table manners are to be observed every time you eat, whether this is at a fancy wedding, your granny's kitchen, or at the Cracker Barrel. I have survived many intimidating dinners and navigated many elaborate table settings by relying on the knowledge I acquired in debutante training. I went through a small town debutante program that was not predicated on your family's prestige or wealth—if you weren't in jail or pregnant, you qualified. Nevertheless, I was taught the same table manners as high-society Southern debutantes: don't drink from the finger bowl, never place used flatware on the table surface, don't use the linen napkin to remove your lipstick, and the most important rule of all: do not begin eating until everyone at the table has been served.

You must also never use a toothpick at the table. Do y'all hear me?

Furthermore, you must place your napkin in your lap, keep your elbows off the table, sit up straight, and chew with your mouth closed. You always pass to the right and you never divorce the salt and pepper shakers—even if the person who only requested the pepper is in the midst of a heart attack. You must never reach across the table and eat off of another person's plate like a wild animal, and you should never discuss religion or politics at the dinner table. You must also never use a toothpick at the table. Do y'all hear me? Never. Even if you have a bacon cheesesteak melt hung up all in your molars at the Waffle House. It looks low rent—and you should never look low rent even if you can't afford your rent.

Social Graces

Even if you master politeness, kindness, and table manners, you will be denied a degree in Southern charm unless you become proficient in social graces. I must warn you this is the most exhausting fundamental. Many Southern boys attend cotillion classes to learn social graces such as social dancing. But social grace training is much more complex for females. Long before Southern girls are old enough to go through the charm schooling required for cotillion or debutante, they are enrolled in Dolly Dinkle Schools. These are schools of tap, ballet, jazz, gymnastics, clogging, music, voice, pageantry, modeling, fire eating, baton twirling, pom-pom shaking, and parade float riding—all skills meant to foster social grace and potentially land you in the Miss America Pageant.

When I was two and half years old, Mama began my Miss America training by enrolling me in Miss Marion's School of Dance. Mama was not deterred by the fact that she could not afford the lessons. Sacrifices must be made in the name of social grace! So Mama took a side job working at Miss Marion's and saw to it that I studied every form of dance. Other lessons followed: piano, voice, banjo . . . Mama was determined for me to have a sensational talent routine prepared for my inevitable participation in Miss America.

Of course, you can't possibly win Miss America without years of pageant training, so Mama got on top of that as well. I won my first pageant title, "Wee Miss Gaffney," when I was five years old. I participated in hundreds of pageants and was coached by various Southern pageant experts, like Rita Allison, who worked diligently to correct the unfortunate fact that, due to my ballet training, I walked turned out like a duck. Interview skills were honed, charity work was encouraged, smiles were perfected, gliding across stages in layers of twinkle material was cultivated, dancing in eighty pounds of ruffles and sequins became second nature, and losing with grace was refined. I'm an excellent loser.

The irony is after all the pageants, Dolly Dinkle Schools, and debutante training, I graduated high school with zero interest in pursuing Miss America. Mama is still recovering from this news. But learning to smile under pressure, hold my head high and my shoulders back, remain poised in the spotlight, speak knowledgeably about current events, complete a routine or task despite making mistakes, and having the ability to glide across any surface without resembling a duck are all social graces that have served me well, both socially and professionally.

I would rather be accused of being a devil worshiper than tacky.

Due to my career, I don't currently have the privilege of living in the South, but the South follows me everywhere I go. I strive to be polite, kind, mannered, and display the social graces that were instilled in me. I will never chew gum in public, get a slutty tattoo, or give a limp-noodle handshake. I home-cook meals for guests and immediately offer anyone who enters my home something to drink or eat to make them feel welcome. And I will never show up to a dinner party without a "happy," which is a hostess gift, because to do so would be tacky beyond words. Like most Southerners, I would rather be accused of being a devil worshiper than tacky. Pursuing a degree in Southern charm teaches you "how to do" and knowing "how to do," is a far more valuable education than any slick Ivy League institution can provide.

Pretty is as pretty does.

GOOD MANNERS NEVER GO OUT OF STYLE.

Can you believe that b*%ch didn't write a thank-you note?

Hospitality is making your guests feel at home, even if you wish they were.

CHARM IS MAKING THE POOR FEEL RICH AND THE OLD FEEL YOUNG.

It's best to measure charm
so you don't drown
in your own sweet tea.

A GOOD ATTITUDE SPREADS LIKE KUDZU.

It's ill-advised to be ill-mannered, ill-dressed, or ill-informed.

Sweetie, your cell phone was not invited to dinner.

Good manners are not to be taken on and off like pearls.

The most valuable item in your wardrobe is your smile.

Always leave your house clean in case you die.

Being real doesn't dictate being rude.

KINDNESS IS NOT PREDICATED ON YOUR MOOD.

Charm disarms.

Having no manners
is worse than having no money.

*There's nothing tackier
than being tacky.*

SHE'S SO TACKY SHE CHEWS GUM IN THE CHOIR LOFT!

She's so tacky she
puts on lipstick at the
dinner table!

Can you believe she
showed up without calling?

IT'S RUDE AS CAN BE NOT TO RSVP!

Cleavage is an evening accessory.

KEEP BOTH FEET OUT OF THE GUTTER.

If Mama wouldn't approve it, don't post it.

Don't go from debutante to double-wide.

There is never an excuse for bad manners.

THANK YOU, SUGAR!

Excuse me, darlin'.

YOU'RE AS WELCOME AS SWEET 'TATER PIE!

When dancing the man leads, when dining the host leads.

When in doubt ask folks about their favorite subject . . . themselves.

Never let on how bored you are.

DON'T SPEAK WITH YOUR MOUTH FULL, ESPECIALLY WHEN IT'S FULL OF BULL.

Good posture speaks louder than your resume.

Never underestimate the power of inner sparkle.

HORSES SWEAT, SOUTHERN LADIES GLOW.

Southern ladies don't get drunk, they get over served.

SOUTHERN LADIES DON'T SMOKE IN PUBLIC.

Southern ladies don't sit with their legs spread wide as Texas.

Talking ugly makes you ugly.

A WHISTLING WOMAN AND A CROWING HEN ALWAYS COME TO NO GOOD END.

Always be aware when you've had a gracious plenty.

GOOD MANNERS ARE FREE, BUT FORGETTING THEM COSTS YOU DEARLY.

Talk Southern to Me 'Bout Beauty and Style

Beauty and Style

"Pearls go with everything except a thong bikini."

Southern women are renowned for their beauty and style. The moment they fly outta the womb, their Mamas teach them to take care of themselves and to always put the "appropriate" amount of time into their appearance. My Mama worked very long hours at two jobs, yet she never failed to get up at the crack of dawn and spend no less than an hour getting beautified for work. Come to think of it, I've seen her spend equal time getting dressed for the drive-thru at Rite Aid. Her favorite item on earth is her makeup mirror, where she can scrutinize her cosmetic skills in "home," "office," and "evening" illumination. She refuses to travel without her makeup mirror—given the painful choice she would rather leave behind my Daddy.

And I must admit, the pecan didn't fall far from the tree. My favorite toy as a child was Mama's big jar of Nivea face cream. I would spend hours sitting on the bathroom countertop applying it to my face and pretending to be the spokesmodel in a commercial for the product. I remember sitting in a Shoney's Big Boy booth in the sixth grade and tearfully begging my parents to let me shave my legs because I simply couldn't bear the humiliation of going through life one more day with hairy legs. And I was ecstatic when I received an entire case of VO5 hairspray for Christmas in high school. A case, y'all! Of course, it was all used up by February. Oh and I will confess that I currently own no less than sixty-three tubes of lipstick.

Let me be clear, this madness never ends. The older a Southern woman gets, the more she becomes obsessed with her appearance. This is why the little old ladies at the assisted living facility regularly get their hair dyed, are fixated with their "casket outfits," and make late, showy entrances to afternoon bridge games. It's better to arrive late than ugly.

Southern men get second billing in this department, but they, too, are taught from a young age how to put themselves together. Think of the ranch worker's cowboy boots, politician's bow tie, drunken frat boy's khakis, or working man's flannel shirt. Whether rugged, conservative, preppy, or country, Southern men have style. And even though Southern men complain about how long it takes us women to get ready, they secretly appreciate the passionate effort we make.

Now, of course, we Southerners realize that character and spirit are the true measures of beauty, but this does nothing to deter our infatuation with outer elegance. Southern women love makeup, and going out in public without it is not an option. We wear it everywhere: the grocery store, the gym, the pool. We hone our skills and can apply it perfectly while whizzing down a lake on a speedboat. Our secret for setting makeup is to spray it with hairspray. Yep, we even use hairspray on our faces.

And speaking of hairspray, whether you're a pageant queen, a nurse, or a lawyer, if you're Southern, you care a lot about your hair. We will spend our very last dime on it if necessary. We believe there is never an excuse for bad hair, which is why Southern hairstylists have bedridden clients. And don't think Southern men can't be hair obsessed. I've met men who would rather cut off their hand than their mullet. And have you heard of the preppy Southern boy swoop cut? Look it up—it has swept the South.

Southern women also treasure their glowing skin. Luckily, the humidity helps preserve our skin, but we are militant about our skincare regimens. We apply moisturizer every night of our lives, even if we drank too much white Zinfandel to remember that we did it. And we care as much about the state of our nails as the state of the Union. Regular manicures and pedicures are a given, as no Southern woman worth her salt runs around with mangled hands and toes. We also understand the allure of a signature smell. We experiment with perfumes, figure out what works, apply a delicate amount, and stay loyal to it for years. I've been wearing the same gardenia scent since 1996.

We care as much about the state of our nails as the state of the Union.

Southerners also have some very particular fashion protocols. We would rather eat fire ants than get caught wearing white after Labor Day or before Easter. We monogram everything except our pets, and there's probably a Southerner out there who's done that. Whether fake or real, Southern women love pearls and wear them everywhere from the country club to the tractor pull. A sorority sister once told me, "Pearls go with everything except a thong bikini."

Southern women love to flaunt their femininity. We know there is nothing more polished, sophisticated and powerful than a smart dress and nothing tackier than an ill-fitting one. And we Southern women "get our colors done" professionally, so we know our most complementary shades. We love to be the center of attention, and know that you can't stand out in a crowd if you're wearing depressing, boring black. We save black for funerals. And we love sparkly stuff. Our closets tend to look like someone vomited rhinestones. Our jewelry boxes, containing both costume and real pieces, can be as big as a pickup truck. Bottom line is, Southern women love to shine bright and we couldn't care less if we blind you in the process.

Southern folks live in linen, lace, floral prints, polka dots, seersucker, plaid, flannel, and of course, gingham. It doesn't bother us at all to dress like a picnic table. Then, of course, there's camouflage, which is not reserved for hunters and military folks. In the South, camo is a fashion choice, and not just for men. Women wear it too, especially in pink.

Southerners also appreciate the value of a good bow. Bow ties have never gone out of style down South and men wear them in an array of fun fabrics tied with perfect precision. And gigantic hair bows are stuck on the heads of little Southern girls from infancy. Everybody down South knows the bigger the bow, the more your Mama loves you.

The bigger the bow, the more your Mama loves you.

And it only takes one trip to the Kentucky Derby to realize that the crowning glory of a Southerner's outfit is a standout hat. Southern women are renowned for wearing wide-brim hats. Cowboy hats are beloved by both men and women. And although Southern gentlemen look dapper in fedoras, they are famous for their endless collections of baseball hats.

I would be remiss not to mention the Southern infatuation with jeans and cowboy boots.

It doesn't matter if our jeans are generic or designer, bootcut or tapered, stiff or stretchy, Southerners *love* their jeans. And cowboy boots are not just to be worn with jeans. We wear them with dresses, shorts, tailored suits, wedding gowns, swimsuits, tuxedos, bridesmaid dresses, and pajamas.

All this intense effort we Southerners put into appearance is often mistaken for vanity, but it is not about vanity at all. Being "well put together" is about respect: respecting yourself by always marketing the most dignified, confident you regardless of your budget; respecting the assets you have been given and making the most of them; respecting the occasion by arriving well groomed and wearing something suitable; respecting the Lord by not dressing like you're for sale; and respecting your kinfolk by not embarrassing the fool out of them by wandering around Dillard's in your tackiest sweatpants.

IS THIS TACKY?

You can't wear that; it's inappropriate!

You're gonna get old and new-monia dressed like that.

I WOULDN'T WEAR THAT TO A DOG FIGHT.

His pants are so tight if he farts his shoes'll fly off.

You'll feel better if you slap on a little lipstick.

You can tell a lot about a person just by looking at their fingernails.

THAT BLOUSE IS UGLIER THAN HOMEMADE SIN.

If it can't be monogrammed, I don't want it.

You gotta get gussied up!

My hair is so big
it's got its own zip code.

These earrings sparkle like a diamond in a goat's butt!

Sugar, just 'cause it zips don't mean it fits.

NEVER WEAR FIVE DOLLARS WORTH OF TEN-CENT MAKEUP.

Put on some makeup; you look like death on a cracker!

I look like something that's been chucked out the side of a lawn mower.

YOU LOOK PRETTIER THAN A SPECKLED PUP!

The higher the heels, the lower the morals.

She's wearing last year's jeans in this year's butt.

My hair is flat
as a flounder.

THAT SUIT'S UGLIER THAN A BOWLING SHOE.

I need to put some
paint on this barn.

Lord, if them britches turn loose,
all her gravy's gonna run out.

**These pants
pick up everything but
men and money.**

I'M GONNA TEASE MY HAIR 'TIL IT CRIES.

My fake eyelashes are so big, if I blink I'll take flight.

That dress makes your butt look like a truck full of cantaloupes.

Camo is my signature color.

My hair looks like it's been pulled through a chicken fence backwards.

Now, who let her outta the house lookin' *like that?*

That bow doesn't match that outfit.

Beauty is skin deep but ugly is to the bone.

His pants are so tight he had to jump off a building to get in 'em.

NEVER STUFF 20 POUNDS OF 'TATERS IN A TEN-POUND SACK.

Lord, everything she's got is out on the show room floor.

MY HAIR IS STANDING FORTY WAYS TO SUNDAY.

Honey, that hat is the berries!

I can't have surgery 'til I touch up my roots.

Always wear clean underwear in case you're in a car accident.

Always flaunt your femininity.

Lord, she's had that weave in since Jesus was a baby.

The higher the hair, the closer to God.

HER PANTS ARE SO TIGHT I CAN SEE HER RELIGION.

You look prettier than a store-bought doll!

I was on my way home but then something sparkly caught my eye.

You look like something the dog keeps under the porch.

Hun, you don't wanna be wearing that when Jesus comes back.

If you can get dressed for Saturday night you can get dressed for Sunday morning!

I'VE TALKED ALL MY LIPSTICK OFF!

Talk Southern to Me When Chewin' the Fat

Chewin' the Fat

"Some of the butter has slid off her biscuit."

Anybody who's ever met a Southerner knows that we can talk the ears off a hobbyhorse. We're long-winded by nature. In fact, I would venture to say that the only thing we enjoy more than good food is good conversation—we literally chew the fat while "chewing the fat." Now, a good chewing the fat session usually includes some friendly chitchat, a tall tale or two, and of course, gossip. Although we Southerners don't like to admit it, all of us, even the most religious, tend to have something to say about someone and have been known to lend an enthusiastic ear to get the scoop. If a Southerner says, "I don't mean to sound mean, but . . . " you're about to hear something that'll make you drop your teeth.

The problem is that we Southerners are taught from birth to be polite—even if it kills us. So when Southern folks gossip, they have to somehow find a way to maintain an ounce of the politeness that's been drilled into them. This is what I call the art of *Southern snark*. Language is such a vibrant part of Southern culture it's no wonder we excel at crafting colorful insults. But in order to make ourselves feel less evil about making a snarky comment, we utter the three words that are guaranteed to be the most confusing of all to a non-Southerner, "*Bless your heart.*"

Now proper heart blessing requires skill, as the undertones and nuances of this phrase can be perplexing to navigate. For example, this phrase can be used in earnest sympathy such as, "Bless her heart, she just buried her Daddy and now she's eat up with the gout." Or this phrase can be used to indicate, "Thank God it's you and not me," such as, "Your house has termites and your teenager is pregnant? Well, bless your heart." It can mean, "You're a flaming idiot but I'm too polite to say so," as in "You're in pain from your latest round of lipo-suction? Bless your heart." But this phrase packs the most punch when we use it to alleviate our guilt about gossiping and to soften the blow of delivering stupendous Southern snark, like, "Bless his heart, he's so dumb, if brains were dynamite he wouldn't have enough to blow his nose." I realize such warmhearted meanness is confusing and contra-dictory, but it makes perfect sense to us Southerners.

While "bless your heart" is arguably the South's most popular gossip diffuser it is by no means the only one. Another common expression is *"I'm just sayin'."* This phrase allows a Southerner to feel open minded while simultaneously being judgmental. For example, "If she wants to wear white at her wedding, that's her business—I'm just sayin' that woman's seen more ceilings than a house painter." And oftentimes it's used as a thin disguise for envy, such as, "I'm just sayin' I can't believe they spent all that time and money building that humongous house and didn't even bother to hire a landscaper." It's also routinely used when a Southerner has been proven wrong while disparaging someone but can't bring themself to admit it. For instance:

HUSBAND: Did you see our fool neighbor got chickens? That city slicker doesn't know the first thing about raising chickens!

WIFE: Well, you've got a yard full of ducks that refuse to swim.

HUSBAND: I'm just sayin'!

Perhaps one of the South's most brilliant gossip qualifiers is *"God love 'em."* I was raised a Baptist in the Bible Belt and this phrase was as common at church potlucks as CorningWare. For example, "Poor old Buford. His lazy grandchildren are gonna suck him dry of all his money. God love 'em." And I've personally had some version of this warning whispered in my ear at many a potluck, "Do not eat Nettie Mae's lemon pound cake. She insisted on bringing it, God love her, but her pound cake is always off." And I've lost count of how many times I've heard, "God love him, that man's so mean he's going to hell on a scholarship." As you can see, this is an extremely useful adage when a Southerner spews criticism but at the same time is grateful that God loves the victim of the criticism. God love 'em . . . 'cause somebody's gotta.

I would be remiss if I didn't mention my Granny Fowler's favorite Southern snark sanitizer, *"I'm gonna pray for her."* Granny Fowler was a strong, hardworking, kind, classy, charitable, and religious Southern woman who taught Sunday school most of her life. She used to preach, "A dog that brings a bone will carry one." This basically means if somebody comes to you with gossip then they will carry their tendency to gossip elsewhere and talk about you. She knew that the Lord frowned upon the destructive force of gossip and did her best to live like Jesus, but Granny was also human, so sometimes she slipped.

"I'm gonna pray for her."

If Granny had something ugly to say about someone, she was careful to frame it like this: "That woman hasn't worn a napkin's worth of clothes since her divorce. I'm gonna pray for her." Or, "That man's so negative he'd depress the devil. I'm gonna pray for him." And there was nothing worse than when Granny hurled this particular phrase directly at you, "Julia Fowler, I heard you went out on a date with that hooligan Ronnie Haggarty! I'm gonna pray for you."

Granny made it her business to protect my reputation as well as her own, because in the South everybody tends to know everybody, so gossip spreads faster than kudzu. But despite Granny's best efforts, she once found herself in serious danger of being the topic of town gossip. Granny agreed to babysit her uncle Gene's pet myna bird while Gene was out of town. Myna birds are talking birds, and they learn to talk by imitating the words and conversations they hear from their owners.

Granny brought the bird home one night and went to bed early because the next morning she was hosting Bible study at her home. As she cooked breakfast and prepared for her church guests, she began talking to the bird and was tickled she taught it to say things: "I'm making biscuits . . . I'm frying bacon . . . I'm hosting Bible study." When her Sunday school class arrived, Granny bragged to the church ladies about how quickly the bird had learned to imitate her.

Just as she began to lead the Bible study, the phone rang. Granny decided to let it ring because she didn't want to interrupt the lesson. And that's when the bird started hollering, "Sheeyut the phone's ringing! Answer the dayum phone! Somebody answer the dayum phone!" As you can imagine, Granny was totally embarrassed and the church ladies were horrified. Granny finally answered the phone so the bird would stop cussing and she attempted to resume the Bible study. But it wasn't long before the phone rang again and the bird went nuts again, "Sheeyut, will somebody answer that dayum phone! Jesus!" Granny wisely took the phone off the hook and scrambled to explain that the bird was her uncle's but realized this only verified that the bird was technically family, so unfortunately Granny was further humiliated.

Granny told me that after that incident she got several sideways

TALK SOUTHERN TO ME WHEN CHEWIN' THE FAT

glances around town and in church. She didn't know for certain what the church ladies said about her, but she was keen enough to know that stories like that travel faster than lightning. Don't worry, Granny. You keep resting in peace. Even if the church ladies did spread the gossip about your cussing bird . . . I bet they prayed for you.

That woman's so annoying she could raise a stye on a pigs ass.

That man would pull up a sign and argue with the hole.

SHE SHOULD JUST SKIP THE PLEASANTRIES AND STRAP A MATTRESS TO HER BACK.

There she goes,
ass swinging like church bells
at Easter.

He's so dumb it took him three days to study for a urine test.

SHE'S SO DUMB SHE SITS ON THE TV AND WATCHES THE COUCH.

He's so dumb he could throw himself on the ground and miss.

SHE'S DUMBER THAN A BOX OF HAIR.

She's so fat when she hauls ass she has to make two trips.

She's so skinny she's gonna fall through her butt and hang herself.

He's so dumb he couldn't pour piss out of a boot with instructions on the heel.

She don't have all her chairs in her parlor.

His cornbread's not done in the middle.

THAT MAN'S ONLY GOT ONE OAR IN THE WATER.

She's *nuttier* than a fruit cake.

She's not even a hot mess . . .
she's a lukewarm mess.

He's so lazy, sweat won't run off his head.

She's so lazy, she wouldn't work in a pie factory licking spoons.

Her nose is stuck up
so high in the air she could
drown in a rainstorm.

I'D LIKE TO BUY THAT MAN FOR WHAT HE'S WORTH AND SELL HIM FOR WHAT HE THINKS HE'S WORTH.

That woman's
wound up tighter than an
eight-day clock.

THAT WOMAN WOULDN'T WARM UP IF SHE WAS CREMATED.

He's meaner than a sack full of rattlesnakes.

She's so ugly if she wore a stamp nobody would lick her.

He's so ugly he'd scare a buzzard off a gut pile.

HIS BREATH SMELLS SO BAD IT COULD MAKE A FUNERAL TURN UP A SIDE STREET.

That woman talks enough for four sets of teeth.

That man could talk the balls off a pool table.

Her face looks
like she was weaned
on a pickle.

I WOULDN'T TRUST
THAT MAN IF
HIS TONGUE CAME
NOTARIZED.

He's so crooked
if he swallowed a nail he'd
spit up a corkscrew.

That woman's full of more crap than a *constipated* elephant.

That man's slicker than pig snot on a radiator.

HE'S AS USELESS AS A MILK BUCKET UNDER A BULL.

She's as sorry as a two-dollar watch.

She's so sorry
I wouldn't wave to her if
my arm was on fire.

She was so drunk she was stumbling around like a blind mule in a pumpkin patch.

He was so high
he could sit on Wednesday
and see both Sundays.

THAT WOMAN'S GOT MORE ISSUES THAN *BETTER HOMES AND GARDENS.*

That man would complain
if you hung him with a new rope.

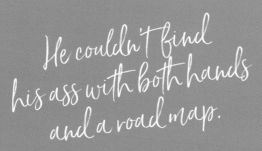

*He couldn't find
his ass with both hands
and a road map.*

The only culture
that woman will ever have
is a yeast infection.

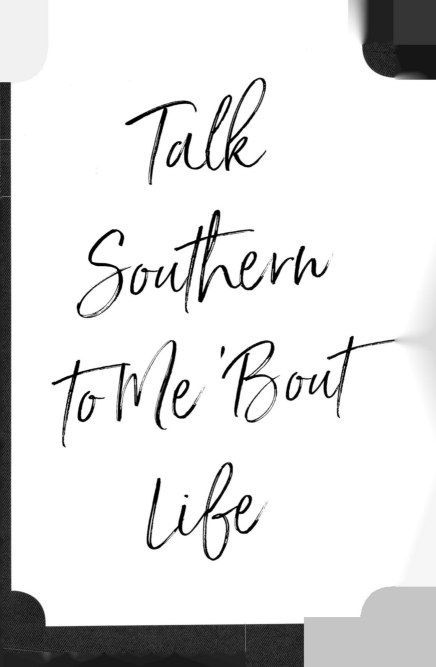

Talk Southern to Me 'Bout Life

Life

"Sometimes you gotta hang in there like a hair in a biscuit."

I was in Philosophy 101 class at the University of South Carolina listening to my professor prattle on about the merits of famous philosophers such as Plato, Aristotle, and Socrates when it dawned on me that I had been raised by philosophers. Being taught "Southern philosophy" is a rite of passage in the South. Southerners have their own particular system of philosophical thought that's not always rooted in formal education but rather in life experience. And that life experience is passed down from generation to generation. And although much of this philosophy doesn't make a lick of sense to us in childhood, as we grow and begin to view life through the prism of adulthood, we come to appreciate the tremendous value of this home-spun Southern wisdom.

My granddaddy, who I called "Papa Cooter," was a cattle farmer, an auctioneer, and a war hero. Now, Papa Cooter wasn't eat up with book smarts, but he was certainly eat up with life smarts. He was diagnosed with Parkinson's disease when I was young and lived with my family for many years, so I got a full dose of Papa Cooter's philosophy. He used to say, "Never kick a cow turd on a hot day." As a kid, I thought to myself, "Why on earth would ya kick a cow turd?" Later in life I understood the lesson he was teaching me—timing is everything. I also came to learn that this was a quote attributed to former President Harry Truman, who, like Papa Cooter, had a grounded sense of philosophy informed by years spent on a farm.

Lord knows I couldn't have been farther away from a farm when I moved to New York City to pursue Broadway. I was young and naïve and had to navigate my way through that urban jungle and all of the dangers that lurked within it. I attribute my survival to the treasure chest of Southern philosophy accumulated from family folks like Papa Cooter. When I first landed in NYC I had a sublet apartment, but the term was only for a month, so time was a-tickin'. I knew I had to immediately hunt for a place to live and thought, "How hard can it be? My cousin Billy and Uncle Jimmy are first rate deer hunters—hunting's in my blood. Hunting comes natural to Southerners." It only took a skinny minute for me to learn that getting an apartment in New York City is more competitive than a Texas beauty pageant.

Now this was back before the Internet, so the apartment listings were in a weekly newspaper called *The Village Voice*. I would run to a newspaper kiosk at dawn to purchase the latest edition, encouraged by my Daddy's motto, "Luck favors the backbone, not the wishbone." I would immediately scour the classifieds and begin the grueling process of calling and setting up appointments with people looking for a roommate or with real estate brokers showing available apartments. Then I would haul my tail all over the city meeting weirdos I could never live with in spaces that were either uninhabitable or outrageously expensive and were usually taken by the time I got there anyway. And the real estate brokers were all slicker than snot on a doorknob. They were fast-talking Yankee sharks whose fees were 15 percent of the yearly rental rate, and that fee was required on top of two month's rent and a security deposit.

The hunt had to be repeated each day, and there was no amount of deer corn that could help me attract an NYC apartment. Every morning began with such optimism and every evening ended in despair. How would I ever make it to Broadway if I couldn't even find a place to live? I went to bed night after night crying crocodile tears but found strength in the philosophical words of my Granny Winnie, "Sometimes you gotta hang in there like a hair in a biscuit."

Sure enough, Granny Winnie was right. Mere days before my sublet was up, I met a lady who had an enormous, sprawling, stunning apartment. She was a widow whose husband had recently died. She said she liked to spend most of her time at her house in the Hamptons, so she was looking to rent one of her bedrooms to someone who could house-sit, since she was hardly ever at her city apartment. Not only was my hunt a success, I had broken the Boone and Crockett Club record! Score! I quickly wrote her a check for nearly half the money I had saved teaching dance back home in South Carolina and skipped through the streets of Manhattan happier than a tick on a hound dog.

I moved into this gorgeous apartment and was so relieved I could finally focus all my energy on getting a job. Unfortunately, this lady focused all her energy on me. She never went to her Hamptons house. In fact, she barely left the apartment. She had everything delivered: groceries, dry cleaning, medicine. I caught her listening to my phone conversations. She rearranged my food in the cabinets and refrigerator. She plastered "No Smoking" signs on my bedroom and bathroom door. I reminded her I was not a smoker. But she insisted the signs were necessary, "In case I had a visitor."

Well one afternoon I did have a visitor. A friend of mine worked on a cruise ship and it was docked in Manhattan for the day, so we went to dinner, and then he came over to see my new place. When he left, this lady had a meltdown and said I was never again allowed to have a guest in the apartment because they might "steal something" and that "strangers made her uncomfortable." My childhood friend Leslie had a sassy Southern Mama named MurMur, who used to preach to us, "To argue with a fool makes two." So instead of telling this fool she was overreacting, I quietly retired to my room. And that's when I noticed that the clothes in my closet had been rearranged. My heart sank. I

"There's never enough makeup to hide crazy."

knew I had to immediately find a new place to live 'cause my Granny Fowler had taught me, "there's never enough makeup to hide crazy."

I left early the next morning for an audition and when I got home in the afternoon, two policemen were waiting to inform me the owner was evicting me. I explained that I had paid for three months rent. They explained that my name was not on the lease so I had no legal rights. My jaw dropped . . . I was homeless. The police forced me to pack on the spot and haul my things down to the lobby. I sat on the stoop of that building, incredulous that I was back at square one and not sure what to do. But eventually, I wiped my tears and accepted reality. As Papa Cooter used to say, "Sometimes you gotta lick that calf all over again."

Thankfully, I had a friend from Tennessee, Tabb, who was a dancer in NYC. Being a true Southern gentleman, he rescued me and allowed me to stay in his crowded apartment until I could figure something out. I was determined to find my own place—no more lunatic roommates. I searched for another few weeks, then one day I made an appointment with a real estate broker handling a vacant studio apartment on the Upper West Side. I put on my nicest dress and heels, did full hair and makeup, and took the subway from Tabb's apartment in Queens to Manhattan. New Yorkers were melting from the oppressive summer heat, but being a Southern woman weaned on humidity, I was unfazed and simply applied more pressed powder. I was on a mission.

When I walked into the office, the real estate agent gruffly shooed me towards a chair then yelled and cursed on the phone while I waited. And waited. And waited. As time passed, my red-headed temper began to boil, but I remembered my Mama's philosophical mantra: "You catch more flies with honey than vinegar." When he finally spoke to me, I proceeded to unload every bit of Southern charm inscribed in my DNA. The ruder he was, the nicer I was. Mama always taught me to "Kill 'em with kindness." The more he tried to dismiss me from his office, the more questions I asked him about his life and family. Charm disarms, and I eventually got him under the Southern spell. Despite the fact that he had a huge stack of applications for that apartment and I was the least financially qualified candidate, he became exhausted by my cheerfulness and said, "Fine! If you'll leave so I can get back to work, I'll help you get this apartment."

I had to bust through a lot of red tape, beg my friend's husband who worked on Wall Street to cosign the lease, and make oodles of pleading phone calls to my Daddy, who reluctantly helped me with money, but I got that apartment. It was so small, when you sat on the toilet you had to put one foot in the bathtub, but I was proud as punch of my palace. Despite an army of roaches, I slept like a baby my first night there, feeling as if I had conquered New York. Little did I know I was about to face a mountain of new obstacles trying to make it to Broadway. But a blind mule ain't afraid of the darkness. So I chased my dream with gusto. And when I made it to Broadway, I got that real estate broker tickets.

Don't let your alligator mouth override your hummingbird ass.

The sun don't shine on the same dog's tail all the time.

DON'T GO UP A HOG'S BUTT TO SEE HOW MUCH LARD IS IN A POUND.

Don't bolt your door with a carrot.

Sweep your own back porch before sweeping somebody else's.

SOMETIMES THE JUICE JUST AIN'T WORTH THE SQUEEZE.

The grass is always greener over the septic tank.

No need to fear the wind
if your hay's tied down.

Anyone can eat
an elephant
one bite at a time.

Don't worry about
the mule going blind. Just
load the wagon.

Turnip tops don't tell you the size of the turnips.

Worrying is like a rocking chair:
gives you something to do
but gets you nowhere.

Don't stir up crap
unless you're willing to
lick the spoon.

NO MATTER HOW SLICK YOU ARE, YOU CAN'T SLIDE ON BARBED WIRE.

You plant a butter bean, you get a butter bean.

Live like a peacock: don't ruffle your feathers unless you're prepared to fight.

Don't bring a knife to a gunfight.

EVEN A BLIND HOG FINDS AN ACORN NOW AND THEN.

Many good flowers get chopped up by associating with weeds.

Let sleeping dogs lie.

You can put boots in the oven, but that don't make 'em biscuits.

TEND TO YOUR OWN KNITTING.

DON'T AIR YOUR DIRTY LINEN IN PUBLIC.

Some folks are all hat and no cattle.

When getting your ducks in a row, remember that some may not be your ducks.

If you ain't the lead dog
then don't expect the view to be
a-changing.

*The guilty dog
barks the loudest.*

Everybody walks up fool's hill.

AN OUNCE OF PRETENSION IS WORTH A POUND OF MANURE.

SOME FOLKS THINK COW HORNS WON'T HOOK.

Never wrestle with a pig;
you'll both get dirty, and the pig likes it.

Life is full of folks who want to lick the red off your candy.

Your chickens will always come home to roost.

YOU CAN'T MAKE A SILK PURSE OUT OF A SOW'S EAR.

If you're gonna dance, you gotta pay the fiddler.

If you can't hang with the big dogs then stay on the porch.

If you find yourself in a hole, quit digging.

Don't take any wooden nickels.

NEVER CHEW YOUR CABBAGE TWICE.

Bloom where you're planted.

Talk Southern to Me 'Bout Love and Marriage

Love and Marriage

"Honey, you really crank my tractor."

I am a natural redhead and whiter than a frog's belly. My body is covered with freckles. I had an overbite so bad I could eat corn on the cob through a picket fence. From age twelve to fifteen I had braces accessorized by external headgear that had to be worn twenty-four hours a day. I was 5'9" by the time I was fourteen years old. My boobs were so small they looked like two cherries on an ironing board. And despite being raised on Crisco-enhanced Southern cooking, I was so skinny, if I stuck out my tongue I looked like a zipper. As you can imagine, boys were not easy.

Yet somehow there were boys. And together we stumbled through years of puppy love and awkward dating, honing our ability to navigate the particular protocols of Southern romance. If you've ever dated a Southerner or if you're married to a Southerner then you know we go about love and marriage a little differently than folks in other parts of the country. There are customs. Conventions. Commandments.

THE TEN COMMANDMENTS FOR DATING IN THE SOUTH:

1. Thou Shalt Impress Mama and Daddy Because Family Matters.

You will never have a truly successful relationship in the South if you don't win over your sweetheart's parents. This won't be easy. Southern Mamas ask a million questions and are extremely opinionated and impossible to please. You will never be good enough for their daughter or son. Accept this and move on. Southern daddies are especially protective of their daughters. They think nothing of standing on the front porch with a shotgun while some poor feller picks up their daughter for a date. Do not agitate a Southern Daddy. Fear him and treat him and his daughter with great respect, or he is certain to whip out a can of whoop-ass.

You must win over the rest of your sweetheart's family as well—brothers, sisters, aunts, uncles, first cousins, second cousins, third cousins removed—all of 'em. You must embrace even the most eccentric of relatives and show genuine empathy when Cousin Lurlene rattles on and on about her restless leg syndrome. Oh, and if you make the critical mistake of betraying your sweetheart, then be prepared for his/her entire Southern family to hunt you down medieval army style. They'll make *Game of Thrones* seem like a Disney cartoon.

2. Thou Shalt Be Chivalrous.

When I was a teen, if a boy blew his horn expecting me to come out of my house and hop in his car for a date, my parents would run that heathen off faster than green grass through a goose. My parents taught me to have enough self-respect to be repulsed by men who did not treat me in a chivalrous manner. Southern women love to be treated like royalty. In fact, we demand it. That's why, even in today's fast-paced world, the South still manages to churn out Southern gentlemen. Proper Southern gentlemen hold open doors for ladies, pull out dining chairs for ladies, stand up when ladies leave the dinner table or enter a room, open car doors for ladies, walk closest to the street, hold umbrellas, help ladies take off and put on coats, and even offer up their own coat if a lady is cold.

Even self-proclaimed Southern feminists know this has nothing to do with ability. Of course Southern women can open their own doors, pull out their own chairs, and put on their own coats. We're a distinctly capable bunch. Chivalrous behavior stems from the fact that Southern men value tradition and enjoy treating women in a special way. And as difficult as this is for non-Southerners to understand, Southern women find this treatment empowering. We love it when our men take the lead and behave like they are in charge. That's 'cause everybody in the South knows the women are actually in charge.

3. *Thou Shalt Not Leave Home If It Took You Less Than Five Minutes to Get Ready.*

The South is filled with men and women who are hotter than doughnut grease. So if you're looking for love, it's unwise to go out looking like something the cat drug in. Looking your best requires time, and even the most naturally beautiful Southern women take a decade to get ready. And don't think this doesn't apply to redneck gals. They too will spend an hour painting their nails, fluffing their hair, applying their makeup, and selecting just the right Bocephus T-shirt to attend the dirt track races. Southern men can spiffy themselves up in no time flat, so they spend the majority of their lives asking their female companions, "Are ya ready yet?" My staple answer is, "I just need ten more minutes." This is always a boldfaced lie.

Mama always encouraged me to look my best in public because "you never know who you might see!" Her advice has served me well. I have met handsome men at the airport, the doctor's office, the DMV, the grocery store, the gym, the car wash, at stop lights, even in port-a-potty lines. When I was living in NYC, I came home one night exhausted from a six-hour dance audition and my friend called begging me to travel to the opposite end of Manhattan because we'd not seen each other in a while. I protested. She insisted, and being a Yankee she said, "You don't have to get all dressed up, just come hang out." Even though I was worn slap out, I washed and dried my hair, put on evening makeup, thoughtfully selected an outfit in a shade of blue that complemented my hair, accessorized my outfit, and trekked to a place I had no interest in going called The Bubble Lounge. That's where I met my husband.

4. Thou Shalt Not Chase Men.

"I would love to take you to dinner. Can I give you my phone number?" That's what my husband said to me when I met him. Moron. I replied, "Sweetie, I'm from the South. I don't call boys. Boys call me." Words that Yankee had never heard uttered. He was instantly intrigued. We've been together twenty-one years.

My Mama would snatch me bald-headed if she caught me calling a boy.

In the South it is considered unladylike to call a male you are romantically interested in. I'm not talking about returning a call; I'm talking about initiating a call. This counts for texts as well and requires tremendous willpower. As a teen, my Mama would snatch me bald-headed if she caught me calling a boy. Young Southern gals today may think this is old-fashioned but that's because they don't understand the brilliance of this Southern philosophy. I will spell it out for you youngins: Men do not like to be chased. They are natural hunters. And they crave a challenge. Why are rare antiques, Monet paintings, and European truffles so expensive and coveted? Because they are not readily available! The less available something is the more valuable it becomes. Smart Southern women know their true value and they don't give discounts.

5. Thou Shalt Flirt with Everybody.

Southerners are flirts. We don't discriminate; we flirt with everybody. I'm not talking about seductive flirting; I'm talking about social flirting. We lavishly address everyone as Sweetie, Darlin', Honey, Honeypie, Honeybunch, Shug', Sugar, Sugarfoot, Sugarmuffin' . . . our tongues are so saccharine it's a miracle our teeth don't rot out by puberty. But this is simply how we endear ourselves to folks, and our DNA stipulates that we chat endlessly and pepper our conversations with compliments. So, if you're the jealous type, dating a Southerner can be challenging.

When it comes to seductive flirting Southerners have superhero powers. Our magnolia accents melt hearts, and while this does give us an unfair advantage, our greatest weapon is our warmth. I've noticed in NYC and LA that people go out and stand around posing and peacocking and ultimately come off as aloof and cold. If you're single, try a Southern approach instead. Make eye contact with the person you are interested in for at least three full seconds, flash a pleasant, welcoming smile, then bat your eyelashes and look away. You have now instilled confidence in your object of desire—they feel "seen," have experienced your warmth, and are less intimidated to approach you. If this person does not engage in conversation with you, then they're not interested, so get over it. There are plenty of other cookies in the cookie jar. Sample many flavors, even ones you don't initially think you'd like.

> We don't discriminate; we flirt with everybody.

6. Thou Shalt Not Be a Hoochie Mama.

Southern women are shameless flirts, but the one thing they avoid like the plague is being called a "hoochie mama." Hoochie mama behavior includes dressing scantily, aggressively flirting with taken men, and being sexually promiscuous. Southern men don't take hoochie mamas home to meet their parents. In the South, shacking up with a man you are not married to, or at least engaged to, is still frowned upon. That's because Southern gals are taught from an early age that a man "never buys a cow if the milk is for free." Of course, oftentimes after the man buys the cow the milk dries up, but that is neither here nor there.

My friend Sheila's Southern Mama preached a great mantra: "The best way to not get pregnant is to hold an aspirin between your knees." Words to live by, ladies. Southern belles are taught to value their virginity and to present themselves to the world with dignity and class. It ain't rocket science, y'all. If you want to be considered a potential wife, then don't act like a whore.

7. Thou Shalt Master Adventure Dating.

If your idea of a date is simply drinks, dinner, or a movie, then you're not cut out to date a Southern man. A Southern man might take you hunting, fishing, four-wheeling, whitewater rafting, kayaking, horseback riding, mountain biking, skiing, hiking, or to the shooting range, the driving range, the races, or the rodeo. Southern gals, although feminine, are sporty and outdoorsy, so these kinds of dates come second nature to us.

When I was in college, I was dating a boy from Kentucky, but he had a sneaking suspicion that I was sweet on a boy at College of Charleston. He was correct. Mr. Kentucky decided he needed to take drastic measures to woo me and save our relationship. So he took me on a two-day canoe trip down the Kentucky River. I was required to paddle miles and miles and miles down the river as the sun blistered my lily-white skin. Then we rushed to set up camp before dark,

Running into your exes can either be painfully humiliating or extremely satisfying.

as there were many more miles to canoe the next day. Just as we got our tent up, a rainstorm complete with ear-splitting thunder and dangerous lightning rolled in and proceeded to punish us for ten straight hours. It had not occurred to Mr. Kentucky to check the weather. Oh, and our tent was not waterproof. As I laid in that tent of muddy water, contemplating my obituary, certain I would be struck by lightning, Mr. Kentucky tenderly turned to me and said, "Isn't this romantic?"

8. Thou Shalt Accept that You Will Always Run into Your Exes.

Even cosmopolitan Southern cities like Charleston, Savannah, and Nashville have a small-town vibe, so one of the consequences of dating in the South is that you are bound to run into your exes. Please refer to commandant number three: Thou shalt not leave home if it took you less than five minutes to get ready. There really is a method to our Southern madness.

I speak from experience when I say running into your exes can either be painfully humiliating or extremely satisfying. No matter the case, politeness is in order. "Hey, how are you? It's so nice to see you. How's your Mama and 'nem? Please tell them I say hey." We never let our exes see us sweat. And if they are with their new spouse or kids, we make a fuss over them too. "So, you got married, huh? How wonderful for you both! Are these your kids? They are precious! They look like you just spit 'em out of your mouth." Then we politely excuse ourselves and walk away gloating, "Bet he wishes he had never let me get away," or jealously muttering, "His wife is ugly enough to haunt a motel chain."

9. Thou Shalt Have a Southern-Fried Wedding.

Why *do* when you can *overdo*? No matter if it's at a country church or country club, this is the credo of Southern weddings, which are filled with coveted traditions. First of all, we never plan a wedding during college football season. Never! And the bride wears white even if it's her thirty-third marriage. Southern brides painstakingly contemplate their "colors." Choosing the wrong colors can throw the whole wedding off, as this affects the flowers, invitations, decorations, and bridal party attire. Speaking of, Southern bridal parties are big enough to staff a Walmart. And monogrammed gifts for each and every one of them are customary. Groomsmen often wear light-colored or seersucker suits, and bridesmaids wear the exact same dress and shoes. I tweaked this custom at my wedding and gave each bridesmaid fabric to make a dress in whatever style she preferred. Some thought I had lost my mind, but it turned out to be a big hit.

Southern brides and grooms diligently register for a china, crystal, and silver pattern, and the groom must be present for this decision even though his opinion will be ignored, because the bride has been mulling this over since the first grade. All the bows must be saved from the wedding shower gifts because a bridesmaid must craft a "bow bouquet" for the bride to carry during the wedding rehearsal. Southern women wield a fierce glue gun.

The bride must get a professional portrait done in full wedding regalia so it can be prominently displayed at the wedding reception despite the fact that she will be there live in person wearing the same attire. If the wedding is outdoors, a bottle of bourbon will be buried on the property to ensure good weather, and after the ceremony it will promptly be dug up and consumed, along with a multitude of other cocktails. Unless it's a Baptist church reception, and in that case you will consume enough punch and sweet tea to go into diabetic shock.

There will be a groom's cake, which is a gift from the bride to the groom, and it will be a visually hideous confection paying homage to the groom's hobbies: football, NASCAR, football. The wedding cake itself, often red velvet, will be tall enough to rival the Empire State Building and will be highly scrutinized by the guests—getting this wrong is not an option. I tasted no less than twenty cake and icing flavors from multiple bakers before choosing my cake. I gave the baker and florist a photo I'd cut out of a bridal magazine years before I was engaged so they'd know exactly what I wanted: fluffy green hydrangeas placed between each towering layer. During my first dance with my husband, I saw the cake across the room and IT WAS NOT MY CAKE! There was a delivery mix-up so I had another bride's cake. That thing was ugly enough to blister a mule's ass at forty paces. I 'bout died. In any case, I did freeze and save the hideous top layer until my first anniversary 'cause Mama insisted it would be bad luck if I didn't.

That thing was ugly enough to blister a mule's ass at forty paces.

You'll often see cowboy boots worn with formal attire at Southern weddings, but at my wedding there was another shoe of choice: clogging shoes. We tore up that dance floor with a full-scale hoedown because Southern folks love to cut a rug. And while I was not whisked away in a horse-drawn carriage, this is a popular choice of Southern brides.

If you aren't invited to a prominent wedding in the South, no need to worry, because a half page of the local newspaper will be dedicated to the wedding announcement. It will include every single detail about the wedding including the brand name of the mother-of-the-bride's pantyhose. The best wedding announcement I ever saw ended with "The bride and groom left the reception on a four-wheeler with their new bass boat in tow." A huge picture was included. Only in the South.

10. Thou Shalt Accept that You Will Always Play Second Fiddle to Your Southern Spouse's Parents.

Family comes first in the South. Period. So if you marry a Southerner there are some things you must simply accept. No matter how hard you try, you will never cook as well as your husband's Mama. You can use the same ingredients and method, but your husband will still swear that his Mama's broccoli and cheese casserole is better than yours. His Mama will take pity on you and try to help you, but she too will agree that you simply lack the magical broccoli and cheese casserole touch. Bless your heart. Don't worry, even Paula Dean couldn't make it better than your husband's Mama. That's because when your husband eats his Mama's food he tastes nostalgia, and that's impossible to replicate.

Vice versa, men must accept that they will never hold a candle to their wife's Daddy. Southern gals put their daddies on pedestals and think they are authorities on most every subject. You can't buy a weed wacker, much less a house, without your wife first getting her Daddy's approval. You can spend weeks building a spectacular backyard deck, and when you're finally done and proudly reveal it to your wife, she will inevitably say, "Daddy says pressure treated lumber is bad to crack. You shoulda used redwood."

You're sexier than socks on a rooster.

He's as handsome as a Georgia lawyer.

SHE'S FINER THAN A FROG HAIR SPLIT SIX WAYS.

He's so hot,
I'd bite him on the ass and
pray for lockjaw.

YOU'RE HOT AS A PISTOL!

I bet he's got sugar in his shorts.

She's prettier than a basket of peaches.

He's hotter than fish oil.

I wouldn't kick him outta bed
unless he was better on the floor.

He's hotter than doughnut grease.

YOU BETTER COME GIMMIE SOME SUGAR!

That feller's got an ass
like a forty-dollar mule.

Darlin', you're cuter
than a whole
litter of puppies.

HE'S SO CUTE
I COULD EAT HIM UP
WITH A SPOON!

I could suck the sugar
right off his cheeks.

I'd like
to sop him
up with a
biscuit.

SHE'S CUTER THAN A BUG'S EAR.

I'm gonna climb your frame like a coon climbs a corn stalk.

That gal makes me grin
like a possum
eatin' sweet 'taters.

That boy's got more moves than a slinky going down an escalator.

He's hornier than a three-horned billy goat.

Well, ain't he just the tomcat's kitten.

YOU'LL NEVER FIND MR. RIGHT HANGING AROUND WITH MR. WRONG.

She's so trashy
she better not linger by the curb
on garbage day.

She's anybody's dog that'll hunt her.

Flit around from flower to flower and you wind up an old maid.

WITH GREAT CLEAVAGE COMES GREAT RESPONSIBILITY.

You can't ride two horses with one ass.

If you lay down with dogs you wake up with fleas.

LOVE CAN'T HELP WHAT IT FALLS ON EVEN IF IT'S A PILE OF SH*T.

There's an ass for every seat.

The older the fiddle,
the sweeter the tune.

Sugar, you've still got that new car smell.

I LOVE YOU MORE THAN A PIG LOVES SLOP.

I love you like a coon dog loves hunting.

THAT COUPLE'S TIGHTER THAN BARK ON A HICKORY TREE.

She'd be better off sticking a toothpick in a lion's ass than messing with my man.

Southern women forgive their men when they are safely buried.

There's no difference between a hornet and a yellow jacket when it's in your britches.

You'll never find a rose in a pig pen.

BLUEBIRDS HAVE ENOUGH SENSE NOT TO MARRY BUZZARDS.

A blacksnake always finds his way to the hen's nest.

That man's just another job
that don't pay.

**If he ain't handsome
he better be handy.**

*You can't turn a hoochie
mama into a housewife.*

YOU DON'T HAVE TO
EAT THE WHOLE EGG
TO KNOW IT'S ROTTEN.

If you marry for money you earn every cent of it.

LOVE FLIES OUT THE WINDOW WHEN POVERTY WALKS IN THE DOOR.

If it has tires or testicles it's bound to give ya trouble.

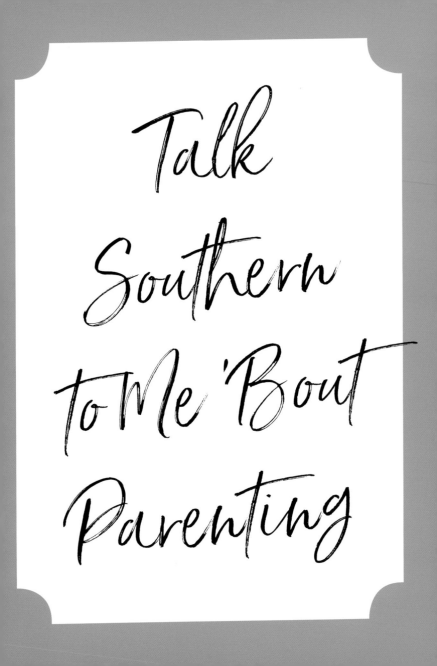

Talk Southern to Me 'Bout Parenting

Parenting

"You can get glad in the same britches you got mad in."

Southern parents are 'bout as subtle as a tornado in a trailer park. They call it like they see it and rarely sugarcoat it. In order to be considered a true Southerner, you gotta be raised by one. I was raised by a village of Southerners: Mama, Daddy, two sets of grandparents, aunts, uncles, teachers, preachers, and babysitters. None of these folks put up with my shenanigans. As a child, I was confused by their quirky philosophies and annoyed by their strict rules. But I now realize I was brought up with tremendous love and wit and am forever grateful that my family molded me into a strong Southern woman with social graces.

Traditionally, Southern children are taught to respect their elders and do not call their elders by their first name. It's always "Ms. Honeycutt" or "Mr. Littlejohn." These are the rules. "Yes, ma'am," and "No, sir" are not optional—these phrases are required for survival. On several occasions I have offended a non-Southerner by saying "Yes, ma'am." And believe me, there wasn't enough time left in the universe to get them to understand I was simply being polite.

A healthy amount of fear is instilled in Southern children. The most dreaded thing Mama could say to me was, "Just wait 'til I tell your Daddy." And all my Granny Fowler had to do was simply cut her eyes at me in church and I knew immediately that I better sit up, shut up, and respect the Lord if I wanted to live to eat another piece of her mouthwatering Minnehaha cake.

Southern children aren't raised in a democratic fashion. They aren't given much of an opportunity to negotiate with their elders. A phrase I heard a million times as a child was, "'Cause I said so, that's why." End of discussion. Bellyaching (aka whining) is frowned upon, and hissy fits, especially in public, are not tolerated. That's 'cause Southern Mamas do not like to be embarrassed in public . . . *ever*. Lord knows, I'm no parenting expert, but I do know that the South has its own particular style of child rearing; a style that I haven't observed while living in other parts of the country.

Here's a li'l story to illustrate my point:

While in a fancy department store in Los Angeles on a crucial mission to find the perfect shade of coral lipstick, I saw a little girl running amuck in the makeup department. She was putting her hands all over the makeup samples, knocking over displays, climbing on the makeup stools, and using the lipsticks as body crayons. We'll call this precious child "Little Miss Nightmare." I thought the weary sales ladies' eyeballs were gonna pop right outta their sockets from holding in their anger.

Now, Little Miss Nightmare's mother was unaware of this madness 'cause she was too busy talking on her phone and puckering her silicone-injected lips in every mirror she encountered. When Little Miss Nightmare sprayed her mother with some foul-smelling perfume, her mother finally took notice and calmly said to her child, "I'm shopping, please behave." That's when Little Miss Nightmare proceeded to have a full meltdown. She threw herself on the department store floor, kicking, screaming, and crying uncontrollably. I watched as the mother casually sampled hand cream and chitchatted with her screaming extraterrestrial.

The mother said, "Tell me what you are feeling." The child squalled uncontrollably. The mother said, "Use your words and tell me what you're feeling." Little Miss Nightmare squalled louder. The mother, who could not have cared less that her daughter was causing a scene, continued this line of questioning, "If you could describe your feelings as a color, what would it be?" To everyone's delight, Little Miss Nightmare squalled *even louder*. The mother casually said, "Try to articulate what would make you feel less distressed." The child replied through sobs and tears, "Chocolate." The mother, still wrapped up in her lotion sampling, said, "You already ate some organic cacao today, remember?" Little Miss Nightmare sobbed and stomped and yelled, "BUT I WANT *REAL* CHOCOLATE!" The mother, who had moved onto eye shadow sampling, said, "We've discussed this. Chocolate is bad for your skin." This sent Little Miss Nightmare into full dying duck fit frenzy mode screaming, "I WANT CHOCOLATE NOW! I WANT CHOCOLATE NOW NOW NOW!!!"

The mother refused to fold on the chocolate, but I'm sure that's because she couldn't bear facing the Los Angeles mommy cliques with a chocolate-eating, sugar-consuming, acne-prone kid. I watched in awe as the mother went into full negotiation mode agreeing to buy something for the child in order to get the kid to calm down. I stood there, jaw dropped, looking like a carp as the mother bought Little Miss Nightmare a tube of Chanel lipstick. *Chanel* lipstick. Good gussie! You can't make this stuff up.

Now, here is how that scenario would typically play out down South.

The very moment the child begins destroying the makeup department, the Southern Mama says sternly, "I've got two words for you: BE-HAVE." The Southern child, being a child, still proceeds to pitch a fit. The Southern Mama narrows her eyes and warns, "Quit actin' ugly." The Southern child, testing boundaries, continues the fit. The Southern Mama, now in full-on embarrassment mode, smiles apologetically to everyone watching then turns to her child and snaps, "Stop making a spectacle of yourself!" The stubborn Southern child's fit escalates. The Southern Mama, now furious, plasters on a pageant

"If you don't stop crying, I'm gonna give you something to cry about."

smile and under her breath through gritted teeth gives the ultimate Southern parental warning, "If you don't stop crying, I'm gonna give you something to cry about." The child immediately calms down, sniffles and says, "I want chocolate." The Southern Mama dryly retorts, "Yeah, well, people in hell want ice water."

Now I'm certain there are plenty of fancy child psychologists who find fault in this Southern parenting style. Nevertheless, this is generally how it's done down South. And we grow up knowing it's rooted in immense love. Funny thing is, Southern parents don't stop raising you just 'cause you grow up or have kids of your own. No, no, no—it never stops. For the sake of sanity, I have learned to never embarrass my Mama in public and have resigned myself to the fact that my Mama's way of doing things will always be better than my way. And I know that my Daddy will forever scold me like a five-year-old if he thinks I am acting meaner than a snake. And yes—Southern adults call their parents Mama and Daddy 'til the day their parents die. And then ironically, they deeply mourn the fact that all that suffocating, supreme Southern rearing is officially over.

Y'all play pretty.

YOU 'BOUT TO POKE SOMEBODY'S EYE OUT!

Bless your little
pea-pickin' heart.

Act like you got some raising!

It ain't dirty.
Just blow it off.

When in doubt,
ask yourself
what Jesus would do.

YOU BETTER MARCH YOUR BEHIND OVER THERE AND APOLOGIZE.

Quit workin' all that devilment!

Never pays to get too big for your britches.

Be home by dark thirty or I'm sending the hounds to look for ya.

Eat this . . . it'll make you pretty.

Suck it up, buttercup.

Stop cuttin' up!

I'M 'BOUT TO JERK A KNOT IN YOUR TAIL!

Idle minds are the devil's playground.

Don't you roll your eyes at me in that tone of voice.

YOU GET WHAT YOU GET AND YOU DON'T THROW A FIT.

You are who you associate with.

Don't act like you were raised in a barn!

Don't you track up my floors!

Just wait 'til your Daddy gets home.

*Did your
Daddy teach you that?*

Get your hind end down from there.

Keep your dress down and your nose clean.

YOUR FACE IS GONNA FREEZE LIKE THAT.

If you don't stop doing that you're gonna go blind.

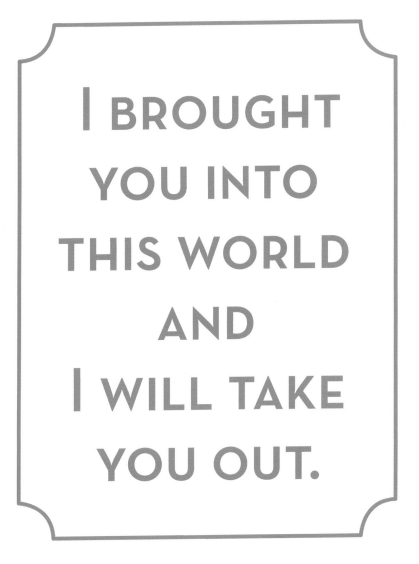

I BROUGHT YOU INTO THIS WORLD AND I WILL TAKE YOU OUT.

You need to drink
some act right juice!

YOU'RE CUTE AS A
BUG IN A RUG!

Life sucks, hun.
Get a straw.

If y'all are gonna kill each
other, then go outside.

Child, you gotta
cowboy up.

Quit wigglin' like a worm in hot ashes.

You need that like you need a hole in your head.

DO NOT BOTHER ME UNLESS YOU'RE ON FIRE.

You didn't get that from my side of the family.

ME AND YOU ARE 'BOUT TO HAVE A COME TO JESUS MEETING.

That's your little red wagon to pull.

No child of mine is going out of the house dressed like that.

Use your head for more than a hat rack.

DON'T YOU BACK SASS ME!

Piss-poor planning on your part does not constitute an emergency on my part.

Get outta that!

YOU GONNA RIDE TO TOWN ON THAT POUTING LIP?

Darlin', you got a caviar appetite on a peanut butter budget.

You better give your heart to Jesus 'cause your butt is mine.

Pee in one hand and wish in the other and see which one gets filled up the fastest.

Can't never could 'til he tried.

YOU'VE MADE ME PROUD AS PUNCH!

You're gonna
miss me
when I'm dead
and gone.

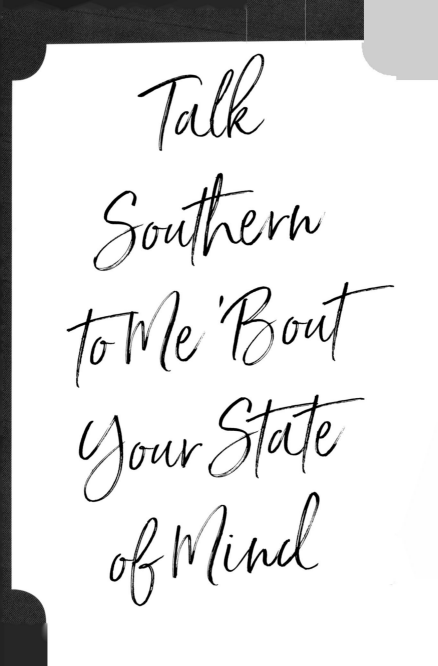

Talk Southern to Me 'Bout Your State of Mind

Your State of Mind

"I'm madder than a cat being baptized!"

Are Southerners more emotionally expressive than people living in the rest of the country? Does a cat have climbing gear? Does a one-legged duck swim in a circle? Does a fat baby fart? Duh! As a matter of fact, I'm downright irritated somebody might think we're not more emotional than our northern and western counterparts. It irks the stew outta me! Makes me wanna slap the taste outta somebody's mouth! Oops. Sorry. My hot-tempered Scotch-Irish heritage is show- ing—I better tuck my tongue behind my teeth.

The irony is that although Southerners are extremely emotional creatures, we are masters at holding our tongues for the time being in order to put on a good face in public. No matter how upset you are at your lazy brother and his wife for mooching off your parents, you will act happy at their Fourth of July lake party on a pontoon boat your parents essentially paid for. Even if your husband informs you he wants a divorce while y'all are driving to the annual church Christmas pageant, you will arrive as the picture perfect couple and stew quietly as you endure amateur actors anointing baby Jesus. Of course, in the long run this only makes things worse. Our tendency to temporarily sweep our emotions under the rug only allows them to fester. Our emotional pot simmers beneath our sparkling, pleasant, pearly white smiles until it erupts with the force of a volcano. Ultimately, Southerners can't hide from their emotional nature.

The Scotch-Irish were early settlers of the Southern United States and brought with them a tough defensive attitude that stemmed from the necessity to safeguard their livestock from rustlers. Some believe this is why Southerners still live by a deep-rooted protective code of honor. Others argue that our emotionally reactive nature is due to the South's warm climate—we tend to get hot under the collar. Many would argue that our tetchiness comes from the burden of history that weighs on Southerners and the amount of suffering we must endure from patronizing non-Southerners. Here's what I know for certain: antagonizing a Southerner is like picking your teeth with a rattlesnake.

I've always battled my temper. But I take some comfort in knowing that I get it honest. My Daddy is a prime example of a Southern hothead. He's a loving, mild-mannered Southern gentleman who has a wonderful sense of humor—until you make him angry; then all bets are off. He transforms into an unrecognizable alien of fury who courteously warns his provoker, "You better give your heart to Jesus, 'cause your butt is mine!" You just never know what might set him off.

A few years ago, Daddy went in for a routine heart catheterization and wound up being immediately prepped for emergency triple bypass surgery. The concerned surgeon popped into Daddy's hospital room and asked, "Mr. Fowler, are you aware you are obese?" Well this sent Daddy into a rage. "What kind of question is that? The very idea! Of course I know I'm fat! I'm not here to get a dayum tooth pulled!" Thankfully, Mama was there to remind Daddy that his life was in the hands of this surgeon, so he best calm his fat ass down.

Daddy's brother, Larry Dean, has the same temper. When I was a kid on vacation at the "luxurious" Viking Motel in Myrtle Beach, South Carolina, my Aunt Kathy made beef stew for supper. I'll never forget Uncle Larry getting madder than a cat being baptized simply because we didn't have any ketchup. In his defense, we were too poor to go out to dinner, so our little home-cooked family motel meals were a "special occasion." But, still . . . Uncle Larry fumed for days over ketchup. Even now, if we bring up this story his face gets redder than ketchup. I'm convinced the origin of Uncle Larry's heart and hypertension problems is dadgum ketchup.

My Mama is a perfect specimen of the paradox that defines Southern women. She's a quintessential Southern lady who can mask her emotions if necessary, but she also has a temper. To this day, my high school girlfriends are still afraid of her. "Don't tell Claudia!" continues to be our gang's motto. Of course, it doesn't help that Mama is a bit OCD when it comes to cleanliness and organization, as that only makes her more susceptible to irritation. For example, Mama organizes Daddy's closet into "yard shirts " and "forbidden shirts." The "yard shirts" are for working in the yard and the "forbidden shirts" are for dinner, church, doctor's appointments, etc. Daddy, of course, mocks her system, so when Mama catches him in the yard wearing a "forbidden shirt," she raises hell like a pig caught under a gate. This woman's blood boils over a shirt. And Daddy's blood boils over her systematic shirt arrangement. It's a combustible situation. I can only pray they don't kill each other over this, because the headline in the local newspaper is sure to read "Southern Town Shattered By Scandalous Shirt Slaughter."

But what makes Southern women sneaky dangerous is the fact that their outrage doesn't always manifest in an obvious, explosive way. Southern women are creative spitfires. Before my parents were married, Daddy sent Mama a dozen roses. At the time, Daddy worked at a Texaco station, and when Mama went by to thank him for the flowers, she found another girl there visiting him. Mama left quietly without causing a scene. After the roses had completely died, she had them delivered back to Daddy with the message "Please shove these up your ass."

Also, back when they were dating Mama spotted Daddy's car in the Hardee's parking lot. As she got closer, she noticed there was girl in the car with him and they were clearly enjoying each other's company.

Hell hath no fury like a Southern woman scorned.

So Mama decided to surprise them. She jerked open the car door, jumped into the passenger seat beside this girl and cheerfully said, "Hey, how are y'all doing?" Daddy was so unnerved, he put his car in drive rather than reverse, jumped the curb and crashed his car into an obstruction. Hell hath no fury like a Southern woman scorned.

After being scorned in college, I made an earnest attempt to tame my temper and enrolled in an anger management course. But even with the tools I acquired, I'm not always successful at wrangling my Southern ferocity. I'm not proud of this fact, but it is a fact nonetheless. Because I'm from Gaffney, South Carolina, when I blow a gasket my friends jokingly say, "Julia's going Gaffney." This happened recently. I was at a beach bar grabbing lunch with my friend Kat when a strange man, we'll call him Drunky McDoo, rolled up and had the gall to stick his grimy fingers in my chips and salsa and help himself to a bite. Remembering my anger management skills, I politely asked Drunky McDoo not to do that again. He then proceeded to knock over my drink. So I took a deep breath and calmly asked Drunky McDoo to please go away.

Instead, Drunky McDoo saddled up in the seat next to me and helped himself to another bite of my chips, dragging the guacamole all into the salsa—my pet peeve. So I sternly said, "Sir, you're drunk and belligerent and I need you to back off." Drunky McDoo spit in my face while responding, "I think you need to back off!" In the blink of an

If a Southern woman says, "Oh, hell no," it's already too late.

eye, I was "Going Gaffney," screaming the words you never want to hear a Southern woman say, "OH, HELL NO!" I jumped up and hollered, "Get away from me right now or I'll knock your teeth so far down your throat you'll have to spit 'em out single file!" He was in total shock that a woman would be so brash. My tirade drew the focus of the entire bar, so, thankfully, the staff quickly responded. The bartenders threw Drunky McDoo out and then the manager amusingly inquired if I had any interest in a job as the bar's bouncer. Please be advised: if a Southern woman says, "Oh, hell no," it's already too late.

Of course, anger is not the only emotion us Southerners theatrically express. Take the popularity of "haint blue" porch ceilings throughout the South. This is a historical, concrete manifestation of fear. These ceilings are particularly prevalent in cities like Charleston, South Carolina, and Savannah, Georgia, because that's where Gullah culture originated. The Gullah people are descendants of African slaves from various tribes who lived in the Lowcountry regions of the Southern United States. In the Gullah dialect, "haunt" sounds like "haint" and Gullah culture asserts that restless spirits known as "haints" can't cross over water. So porch ceilings were painted a symbolic light blue to keep spirits from entering the house. Paint companies capitalized on the South's determination not to have their houses haunted, and nowadays a Southerner can purchase paint in a variety of "Ghostbuster" blue shades to assuage their fear.

Truth be told, we Southerners tend to go over-the-top when expressing a multitude of emotions, and we have plenty of colorful Southernisms to precisely describe how we're feeling. This is easily illustrated on any given Saturday down South during college football season, where one can blatantly observe Southern fans going through a plethora of emotional histrionics. Their team will have them nervous as a frog on a freeway, and then a shocking play will surprise them and they'll scream, "Well don't that just beat a hog flyin'!" They'll be happier than a duck on a June bug right up until the moment their team loses the game with a disastrous play. Then they'll bury their heads in their hands, displaying the kind of visible grief usually reserved for a terminal cancer diagnosis. Clinically depressed, they'll spend the following week moping around, feeling lower than a snake's belly right up until the following Saturday, when they'll return to the football stadium more excited than a granny at a yard sale. And then as sure as death and taxes, they'll shuffle through this gamut of melodramatic emotions all over again.

I'm happy as a pig in slop!

I'm happier than a tornado in a trailer park!

If I were any better
I'd be twins!

If I were any peachier
I'd be cobbler.

I'm happier than a woodpecker in a lumberyard!

I couldn't be happier if butter were fat-free!

I'M HAPPY AS A CLAM AT HIGH TIDE!

I'm happier than a mule in a pickle patch!

I'M HAPPIER THAN A BOLL WEEVIL HIDING IN A TUB OF GRITS!

I'm madder than a skeeter in a mannequin factory!

I'm madder than a mule with a mouth full of yellow jackets!

That just creams my corn!

That really gets my goose!

I'm so mad my hair is on fire!

I'm fixin' to lose my religion!

I'LL KICK YOUR BUTT FROM HERE TO CHRISTMAS AND DARE YOU TO WALK BACK!

I'll slap you so hard
your shirt will roll up your back
like a window shade!

That just burns my biscuits!

I am fit to be tied!

I'M MADDER THAN A WET HEN!

I'll knock you into the middle of next week!

I'm so mad I could chew steel and spit nails!

I'M 'BOUT TO GIVE YOU NINE KINDS OF HELL!

I'll slap you to sleep then slap you for sleeping!

I'VE GOT BEES IN MY BONNET!

That dills my pickle!

That irritates the snot outta me!

CAREFUL, OR I'LL CLOUD UP AND RAIN ALL OVER YOU!

I'm so nervous I'm 'bout to jump outta my skin.

I'm nervous as a chicken covered with mustard.

I'm nervous as a virgin at a prison rodeo.

I'm more nervous than a long-tailed cat on a porch full of rocking chairs.

I'm as nervous as a hound dog trying to pass a peach pit.

I'm sweating like a pig that knows he's dinner.

I'm sweating like a whore in church.

YOU SCARED MY MULE!

You scared the bejesus outta me!

Lord, that would scare
the beard off Jesus!

Oh my stars and garters!

WELL, I'LL BE A SOCH-EYED MULE!

Good gravy!

WELL, HELL'S BELLS!

I do declare!

Well if that don't put
pepper in the gumbo!

Well, I'll be a possum on a gumbush!

Well, roll me in flour and call me fried!

BUTTER MY BUTT AND CALL ME A BISCUIT!

I'm sadder than a store-bought radish.

I'm all torn outta frame.

I'm tore up worse than a soup sandwich.

I'm feeling low as a
toad in a dry well.

I'm sadder than
canned biscuits.

I'M TORE UP FROM
THE FLOOR UP.

I feel like
I've been rode hard and
put up to dry.

I feel like I'm sucking
the hind tit.

I feel like
I've been
chewed up
and spit out.

I'm as confused as orphan on Father's Day.

I don't know whether to scratch my watch or wind my butt.

I'm more confused than a cow in a parking lot!

THAT'S DISGUSTING ENOUGH TO GAG A MAGGOT.

That just makes my teeth itch!

Talk Southern to Me 'Bout Stuff That Needs Interpretin'

Stuff That Needs Interpretin'

"That picture is all cattywampus."

A few years ago I went to Paris, France, and realized that—despite earning As in both high school and college French—the only things I could say in French were "I'll have a cheese omelet, please" and, "Hello, my name is Julia. How are you?" Oh, and I can count to ten and also know tons of French ballet terminology, but that proved to be as useless as a sprig of parsley on a steak. I came to the conclusion that one cannot possibly master another language unless you were raised to speak it from birth or choose to dedicate significant time to a full immersion experience. While I was in Paris feeling vulnerable, confused, and sidelined, it dawned on me that's exactly how non-Southerners must feel when visiting the South—lost as last year's Easter eggs.

Southern folks speak their own variant of the English language, and unless you're a Southern native this can be bewildering. We speak Southern slang in a slow, honeysuckled accent, and sometimes we use bad grammar for dramatic effect. This often results in our being misjudged as ignorant or uneducated. Which really gets my goat 'cause I got smarts real good and so do oodles of other Southerners. But why would I say, "This cellulite cream does not seem to be working," when I can say, "This cellulite cream ain't worth a toot!" Why would I say, "I don't care," when I can say, "Makes no never mind to me." Why would I say, "Is this milk expired," when I can say, "Reckon this milk's any count?"

Our word usage in and of itself baffles those outside the South. A pocketbook is a purse. A toboggan is a knit hat. A cooter is a turtle. A buggy is a shopping cart. Cattywampus means askew. And a Coke refers to all varieties of soda. You addled yet? That means confused.

My husband, who's not from the South, bless his heart and mine, is in a constant state of bumfuzzlement. He graduated from one of New York's most prestigious private prep schools, Trinity, and from Boston University. Yet with all his fancy pants, high falutin' education he still can't understand plain Southern English. He stares at me like a tree full of owls when I say, "Put these socks in the chester drawers." He calls a chest of drawers a bureau. Say who? If I say, "Put some glass in that polar bear's ass," you can bet the farm I'll freeze to death before he realizes I want him to close the window. I once said, "Lemme get back to my rat killing," which means I gotta go, I'm busy, and he actually thought I was killing rats. Idjut! I might as well be married to a Frenchman.

I'm fairly certain my questionable Southern grammar makes my husband's skin crawl, especially when I say my favorite expression, "might could." As in, "We can take the freeway if you want to but we might could get there faster on the access road." That's a service road for all y'all who don't know. And speaking of "y'all," it makes my skin crawl when I hear a non-Southerner use "y'all" for a singular person. Blasphemy! "Y'all" is a contraction for "you all." The apostrophe goes after the "y" and "y'all" is always used to refer to more than one person. "All y'all" is used to refer to a larger group of people. "All y'all's" is plural possessive. I'd be much obliged if all y'all's non-Southern noggins could get that straight.

And I'm fixin' to tell ya that "fixin' to" is said in the South just as often as "y'all." It means I'm getting ready to. As in, "I'm fixin' to grill up some gator," or "I'm fixin' to get ready to get ready," or "I'm fixin' to give him a what for and down the road!" Which means I'm fixin'

Southern talk— particularly backwoods, country as cornbread Southern talk—is a secret code.

to cuss him out. In the South we don't curse. We cuss. But when we're minding our manners and don't want to cuss, we say things like, "Dadgumit," "Dadburnit," or "Dernnation!" My Granny Fowler's favorite words on earth were "I swannie," which is what church-goin' folks say instead of "I swear."

Perhaps the most puzzling thing a newcomer to the South will encounter is that what may seem like an innocuous phrase is actually a sneaky insult. In the chapter on "Chewin' the Fat" I covered some of these phrases, including the most popular, "Bless your heart." But there are others. For example, "Isn't that nice," means "Screw you." "Interesting," means "That's idiotic." And "Y'all aren't from around here, are you?" means "Please take your rudeness back from whence you came!"

Seein' as how the Southern language is so difficult to navigate, I think the United States govern- ment should consider protecting itself against foreign cyber threats by writing all classified information in Southern slang. Think about it . . . even if the hooligan hackers got their hands on classified information, they would never be able to decipher it. Foreign hackers might know how to read English, but I'll assure you nobody's taught Southern slang to the Russians, Chinese, Iranians, or North Koreans—and certainly not to ISIS. Southern talk—particularly backwoods, country as cornbread Southern talk—is a secret code that even the Intelligence community is not intelligent enough to decipher unless they are native South-erners. For example:

Zactly leben days ago whilst I wuz pilifering through my pocketbook, I spotted that skelter-eyed, scalleywag Skeeter Ledbetter, out my winder. That fool was traipsin' slaunchways through my 'mater stakes nekid as a jaybird. I had a dyin' duck fit cuz ole' Skeeter is a bit tetched and pert near always hopped up on white lightning. Bein' a grass widow, and seein' as my naybers wuz outta town, I had to cowboy up and head on out taire by my lonesome to deal with this shindy. I hollered a fer piece, "Skeeter, urine big trouble!" but that rascal just tumped over backerds squarshin' a mess of my 'maters.

About to lose my religion, I chunked a rock dereckly at 'em, but I caint hit the broad side of a barn, so he carried on jes laid up daire playin' possum. As I got right chaire at 'em I tilted my eyes to Jesus to avoid seein' his liddey biddy talleywacker and hollered, "Skeeter, I aim to rang the Shurf if you don't giddup on outta here!" Skeeter, who was clearly in the bag, muttered, "Kin ya dew me a favor and lemme lay here aspel? I's plumb tard."

I sighed and 'ventually said, "Whale, senuous worse for the wear you can lay ahere if yonto but it's fixin' to come up a frog strangler and you're lible to ketch yer death." I moseyed on back in the house shakin' my noggin and mutterin', "I swannie, poor ol' Skeeter's got

> That fool was traipsin' slaunchways through my 'mater stakes nekid as a jaybird.

one foot in the grave and the other on a banana peel."

I think our country's enemies would be confused as all get-out if the government's classified information were written out this way. It's a bona fide strategy all those goobers fiddle farting around up in Congress should seriously consider. Shoot fire! I oughtta just run for Congress. I could represent the Boondocks district! Course, there ain't no tellin' the toll it'll take on me to run for office, but, hey . . . you gotta risk it to get the biscuit. Not to put on airs, but I think this here campaign slogan is pure tee genius:

Make 'Merica Safe Again. #MericasFarnEnemiesCanKissMyGrits

Eh, Lordy, I better skedaddle cause I've got umpteen things to do for this campaign.

I'll have to get up with y'all later. Peace, Love, and Chickens!

Stuff Southern Folks Say that Needs Interpreting

Aholt (hold) *Grab aholt of this railing so you don't fall down the steps.*

Aig (stir up) *Please don't aig him on or he'll drive us all crazy.*

Aim to (intend) *I aim to go to Graceland before I die.*

Ain't worth killing (worthless) *That new quarterback ain't worth killing!*

All vines and no taters (fruitless) *You can't trust him; he's all vines and no taters.*

Back (lick) *Will you please help me back all these envelopes?*

Back talk (sass) *Child, you better think twice before you back talk me!*

Bad to (inclined) *My first husband was bad to drink.*

Bill fold (wallet) *I'm gonna buy Daddy a new bill fold for Christmas.*

Bless out (tell off) *I blessed her out for being mean to my child!*

Bone to pick (issue to discuss) *Listen, I gotta bone to pick with you.*

Boondocks (country) *These people live way out here in the boondocks.*

Britches (pants) *How did you get your britches so dirty?*

Calf slobber (meringue) *I make my pies with four inches of calf slobber.*

Carry (take) *Will you carry me to the doctor?*

Carry on (act foolish) *Stop carrying on in church—you're embarrassing me!*

Chunk (throw) *Stop hogging the ball and chunk it to me!*

Clicker (remote) *Where on earth did you put the TV clicker?*

Cop a squat (urinate outdoors) *Pull the car over; I gotta cop a squat.*

Cow's tail (last) *Hurry, I don't wanna be the cow's tail to this party.*

Crick (stitch) *I woke up with a terrible crick in my neck.*

Crocus sack (burlap bag) *Lord, she'd look better wearing a crocus sack.*

Cut off (turn off) *Please cut off that light.*

Dadnabbit (Damn) *Dadnabbit! I burned my hand!*

Dark thirty (shortly after darkness falls) *You better be home by dark thirty!*

Darken the door (enter) *That heathen's never darkened the doors of church.*

Darn tootin' (affirmative) *You're darn tootin' I'm excited for my vacation.*

Dinner (lunch) *Granny's making fried chicken for Sunday dinner.*

Directly (soon) *I'm leaving now, I'll be there directly.*

Do me up (zip or button) *Honey, will you come do me up?*

Do what? (excuse me) *Do what? I couldn't hear you for the hair dryer.*

Doohickey (object) *This dress has a weird doohickey on it.*

Drop cord (extension cord) *I need a drop cord for these Christmas lights.*

Druthers (desires) *If I had my druthers I'd rather go to Cracker Barrel.*

Duck fit (fit of anger) *He's having a duck fit because he lost his cell phone.*

Dying duck fit (extreme fit) *He's having a dying duck fit over politics.*

Ear bob (earring) *These were my grandmama's diamond ear bobs.*

Falling out (argument) *Those two had a falling out.*

Fiddle fart (wasting time) *Stop fiddle farting around and come help me!*

Figuring (ruminating) *Not sure what I'm gonna do but I'm figuring on it.*

Flap doodle (Damn) *Flap doodle! I stumped my toe!*

Flarity tailed (flared) *I want to wear a flarity tailed skirt to the wedding.*

Flew all over me (angered me) *When she said that, it just flew all over me!*

Flip (crap) *My roses didn't do worth a flip this year.*

Fly flapper (fly swat) *We need to get a new fly flapper for the lake house.*

Forty eleven (large quantity) *I've*

already told you that forty eleven times!

Friday week (next Friday) *Can you babysit my kids Friday week?*

Frog strangler (big rainstorm) *That frog strangler almost flooded the pond.*

Get-out (unit of measurement) *I'm drunk as all get-out.*

Give out (exhaust or fail) *Those cheap blenders tend to give out.*

Go whole hog (go all out) *We're going whole hog for this tailgate party.*

Goober (jackass) *That feller I met at the bar was such a goober.*

Gown tail (pajamas) *Lord, she's out in the yard in her gown tail!*

Grass widow (woman separated from husband) *Poor lady's a grass widow.*

Grocery store feet (dirty feet) *You need to wash those grocery store feet.*

Gully washer (big rainstorm) *Looks like it's coming up a gully washer.*

Hankering (yearning) *I have a hankering for cornbread and buttermilk.*

Hard row to hoe (tough task) *Emory Law School is a hard row to hoe.*

Hear tell (I've heard) *I hear tell the mayor is cheating on his wife.*

Hickeydoodle (object or person) *Old hickeydoodle finally sold his house.*

Hightail it (go fast) *We're gonna hightail it all the way to Panama City.*

Hissy fit (fit of anger) *That child is famous for pitching hissy fits.*

Hissy fit with a tail on it (extreme fit) *She pitched a hissy fit with a tail on it.*

Hitched (married) *We're gonna get hitched next June.*

Hockey (manure) *Careful the grass is full of horse hockey.*

Hogwash (nonsense) *That feller's always talking hogwash.*

Hold ya taters (calm down) *Hold ya taters, I'm on my way!*

Hose pipe (water hose) *I'm watering my flowers with the hose pipe.*

Humdinger (unusual) *She's got a humdinger of a husband.*

Hunky-dory (excellent) *I'm just hunky-dory; how are you doing?*

In the family way (pregnant) *She's not telling people but she's in the family way.*

Itty-bitty (tiny) *These itty-bitty buttons are downright annoying.*

Jeet (did you eat) *Jeet yet?*

Kinfolk (relatives) *I've gotta lot of kinfolk down in Louisiana.*

Knee baby (toddler) *I've known her since she was a knee baby.*

Laid up (lying) *Bless his heart, he's laid up in the hospital.*

Let out (dismiss) *What time does the elementary school let out?*

Libala (likely to) *I better write it down 'cause I'm libala forget it.*

Lick and a promise (hasty job) *I just gave the house a lick and a promise.*

Lightning bugs (fireflies) *The kids are outside chasing lightning bugs.*

Lord have mercy (exclamation) *Lord have mercy, I won the lottery!*

Lunch puppy (glutton) *That lunch puppy ate the whole pecan pie.*

Make no bones (not going to fake*) I'm mad and I'm not gonna make no bones about it!*

Make out like (pretend) *She tried to make out like she didn't know anything.*

Mama and 'nem (family) *How's your Mama and 'nem doing?*

Mash (press) *Dern! I mashed the wrong elevator button.*

'Maters (tomatoes) *Are you growing 'maters in your garden?*

Mess (bunch) *We're frying up a mess of catfish tonight.*

Miller (moth) *Shut the door so the millers don't get in the house.*

Nearabout (almost) *I gotta go to the store 'cause I'm nearabout out of eggs.*

Nekid as a jaybird (totally naked) *I saw him nekid as a jaybird.*

No-'count (crummy) *That no-'count stylist gave me an awful haircut.*

Noggin' (head) *Use your noggin' before you open your big mouth!*

Off kilter (not right) *That feller's always been off kilter.*

Out of whack (doesn't work) *My lower back is all out of whack.*

People (relatives) *Now who are your people?*

Pert near (pretty close) *I'm pert near out of hairspray.*

Peter out (fatigue) *You'd be a good ball player if you didn't peter out.*

Piddlin' (wasting time) *He spent the whole day piddlin' around the house.*

Pilfering (sneaking) *Do not go pilfering around in my closet.*

Playing possum (feigning sleep) *Get up and stop playing possum!*

Pure tee (genuine) *He did it just for pure tee meanness!*

Put on airs (act snobby) *I can't stand the way she puts on airs.*

Put up (can produce) *I'm busy putting up 'maters and cucumbers.*

Raise (lower) *Raise that window down.*

Rarin' to go (anxious) *These kids are rarin' to go to the beach.*

Reach me (hand me) *Reach me those shoes off the top shelf.*

Reckon (do you think) *Reckon that new movie is worth seeing?*

Right good (very good) *This cake's right good, isn't it?*

Rinky-dink (pitiful) *That sure was a rinky-dink carnival.*

Rubbernecking (staring) *There's a car accident, so everybody's rubbernecking.*

Ruckus (noise) *Who's making all that ruckus outside?*

Say who (excuse me) *Say who? I'm confused.*

Scooter poopin' (riding around) *We've been scooter poopin' all over town.*

Set up (thicken) *I gotta make my tater salad so it'll set up by tomorrow.*

Shindig (party) *We're going to a big shindig Saturday night.*

Shindy (disturbance) *There was a big shindy up at the beer joint last night.*

Shine to (like) *I'm starting to take a shine to the new preacher.*

Sight unseen (without looking) *Never buy a car sight unseen!*

Skedaddle (leave) *It's getting dark; guess I better skedaddle.*

Skeeter (mosquito) *These skeeters are eating me alive!*

Slap (totally) *I'm worn slap out.*

Slew foot (pigeon-toed) *It's hard to teach a slew-footed child ballet.*

Smack dab (precisely) *I've got a zit smack dab in the middle of my nose.*

Snockerpussed (very drunk) *That woman's snockerpussed at every party.*

Sorry (useless) *You need to get rid of these sorry scissors and buy new ones.*

Spicket (water faucet) *Make sure you turn that spicket all the way off.*

Spittin' image (identical) *That baby's the spittin' image of his Mama.*

Step-ins (underwear) *I better do some laundry 'cause I'm out of step-ins.*

Stocking feet (sock feet) *It's too cold to go outside in your stocking feet!*

Stomping ground (home) *South Carolina is my stomping ground.*

Sugar (kiss) *You better come give me some sugar!*

Supper (last meal of the day) *Tonight we're having okra for supper.*

Tacky (heinous or shameful) *She's so tacky she makes chicken salad with Miracle Whip.*

Tallywacker (penis) *That little boy can't stop playing with his tallywacker.*

Tarnation (damnation) *What in tarnation did you spill on my carpet?*

Thingamajig (object) *Bring me that thingamajig that peels garlic.*

Tight (cheap) *He's so tight he never goes out to eat.*

Tizzy (uproar) *She's all in a tizzy over her neighbor's loud dog.*

Took sick (became ill) *Poor old Edna took sick over a month ago.*

Took up with (close relations) *I can't believe my ex took up with that tramp.*

Tore up (upset) *I've been all tore up since I lost my job.*

Touched (not right) *That poor old woman's always been a bit touched.*

Triflin' (good for nothing) *You ought not be marrying that triflin' man.*

Tuckered out (tired) *I'm all tuckered out from my big yard sale.*

Tump (turn) *You better tump over or your tan's not gonna be even.*

Umpteen (large number) *I've been to Dollywood umpteen times.*

Unbeknownst (unknown) *Unbeknownst to me, he bought a new boat!*

Uppity (conceited) *She's been all uppity since she won homecoming queen.*

Used to could (previously could) *I used to could do the splits.*

Well, I'll be (surprised) *She got a face-lift? Well, I'll be.*

Weuns (we all) *Weuns are tired of youburning trash in the neighborhood.*

What in the Sam Hill (crazy) *What in the Sam Hill are you doing?*

Whatchamadoodle (object) *Where's the whatchamadoodle for this earbob?*

Whereabouts (where) *Whereabouts do you think you're going?*

White lightning (moonshine) *That feller's white lightning is potent.*

Whomper jawed (misaligned) *My tires are all whomper jawed.*

Wingdinger (atypical) *Lord, this day was a wingdinger!*

Wrecker (tow truck) *I had to call a wrecker 'cause my car broke down.*

Wrench (wring) *Wrench out that mop when you're finished.*

Yonder (over there) *They live down yonder next to the cemetery.*

Youins (you all) *Youins better not set foot on my property.*

Youngin' (child) *I don't know how that teacher puts up with those rotten youngins.*

Acknowledgments

First and foremost I would like to thank the devoted fans of the Southern Women Channel. My most unexpected joy in life is that my YouTube videos have brought so many folks so much laughter. Thank y'all for watching, for writing me, and for celebrating Southern humor with me. Thanks for subscribing to the channel, following our social media platforms, and for insisting I make more videos, because without your support, I would not have had the chance to write this book.

This book definitely would not have been possible without my astute literary agent, Berta Treitl, and her team at Renaissance Literary & Talent. Berta, thank you for finding me on YouTube and persuading me to write a book. Thank you for patiently holding my hand through the process, answering my forty-eleven questions, and staunchly persevering until we secured the right book deal.

My sincere appreciation goes to the entire team at Gibbs Smith for the opportunity to write this book and for loving it as much as I do. To my phenomenal editor, Katie Killebrew, thank you for believing in this book and my vision. Thank you for your guidance, for the creative freedom you gave me, and for trusting my Southern voice even when you could barely decipher it.

God brought my dear friend and publicist Will Armstrong into my life for a myriad of reasons and I'm so grateful. Big thanks to Will and the team at Armstrong Public Relations as well as Shelby "Kentucky" Kisgen at Gibbs Smith PR for all y'all's hard work and enthusiastic support.

My steadfast manager and friend, Cindy Ambers, to say thank you for everything would never suffice. Thank you for encouraging me to write and write and write and to always channel my Southern voice. Your confidence in my talent astounds me. Your ability to coach me through disappointment is invaluable. And bless your heart, you deserve a medal for indulging my long-winded conversational nature. I am extremely grateful to you and the entire team at Art/Work Entertainment.

To my brilliant lawyer Erik Hyman at Loeb & Loeb, thank you so very much for having faith in me, for your trusted guidance, and for interpreting all that dadgum legalese! I pray I become successful enough to buy you a designer seersucker suit, because I know you'd look handsome as a Georgia lawyer in it.

I don't even know where to begin thanking all the phenomenal Southerners who have so graciously donated their time, talent, homes, and wardrobe to help me build the Southern Women Channel. Your hilarious personalities inspire my writing and your Southern spirits keep me from having a nervous breakdown in Los Angeles. I am forever indebted to Katherine Bailess, Sheila Hawkins, Delaine Yates, Logan Browning, Kim Kendall, Chasity Smith, Clarinda Ross, Laura Bell Bundy, Patricia Altschul, Aisha Atkins, Annie Sims, Carsyn Bolin, Sasha Koziak, and Del Shores. I'm sure by the time this book is printed there will be more video participants that deserve my gratitude, so I will thank y'all in advance to avoid being rude as all get-out.

The YouTube channel requires loads of help. I must give a special shout-out to my niece Maya Sokolow who took on the daunting task of organizing my collection of Southernisms and along the way learned to speak "Southern" as a second language. Thank you, sugarpie! You'll be a published writer yourself one day . . . I'll bet the farm on it.

Thanks to Troy Christian for your ridiculous talent, to Jeff Fisher for your versatile talents, and to the wonderful musicians: Barney Malin, Heather Bennet Cibula, and Eli Sokolow. Immense thanks goes to those who have patiently endured my meticulous requests—editors: Michelle Patterson, Jose Salazar, and Lou Baldanza; website designers: Matt Billings and Maurice Martineau, and graphic artist Shana Cinquegrana. And big thanks go to Varthuhi Oganesyan, Amy Clites, Kiara Franklin, and Jessica Hogan for all your help.

To Celia Rivenbark and Delia Ephron, you are both writers that I've admired for many years, so I am much obliged and humbled by your kind endorsements. I must also extend my sincere gratitude to Amy Jackson at UMG Nashville and Sam Haskell for your support. And to the Queen of the South, Dolly Parton, I am tremendously grateful for your support, inspired by your homespun artistry and grace, and so very honored that you even know I exist on the planet Earth!

A heartfelt thank you goes to Howie Deutch and Lea Thompson for generously allowing me to shoot at their horse corral and to Peter and Jen Micelli, Cindy and Craig Block, and Ryan Martin for allowing me to shoot at their homes. And to Mama and 'nem's neighbors on White Oak Road— thanks for putting up with my shooting all over the neighborhood.

Mama and Daddy, this book clearly would not exist if y'all had not conceived me in the South, raised me in the South, and instilled a tremendous sense of Southern pride in my soul. I'm truly inspired by your innate sense of humor that God so graciously sprinkled on me. I so appreciate the sacrifices you both made so I could pursue my dreams in places painfully far away from you. Above all, thank you for your love, for supporting me in all my endeavors, and for your unwavering belief in me. I am eternally grateful for your Southern wisdom that continues to be my life compass.

To the rest of my hysterical Southern family: Kathy, Larry, Billy, Lana, Legend, Jimmy, Linda, Lucy, Page, Brandon, Angela, John Allen, Ward, Joe, Alice, Bill, Christine, Sandy, Jan, Stephanie, Dave, Myrtle, Bam Bam, Sadie, Bo, Sarah, Warren, and especially Granny Winnie, Papa Cooter, Granny Fowler, and Papa Fowler—thank y'all for your love and superb Southern wit. Some of you have passed on, some of you I don't get to see often, but in one way or another you have all shaped my life in ways that will forever leave an imprint.

Ginormous thanks must be given to my husband and tireless head cheerleader, Sam Sokolow. I'm in awe of your love, loyalty, and contagious optimism. Thank you for encouraging my various artistic pursuits and for believing in me even when I don't believe in myself. Thank you for taking off your fancy "Emmy Nominated Executive Producer of Television" hat and working as my one-man band crew. The Southern Women Channel simply could not exist without your generous dedication of time and production expertise. Thank you for championing my Southern voice, for your ability to navigate my quirky Southern nature, and for tolerating my constant criticism of your tacky Yankee ways.

Speaking of Yankees, I must thank my mother-in-law, the brilliant Diane Sokolow, for taking this Southern belle under your wing many years ago, for enduring a million "yes ma'ams," and for mentoring me as a writer. To Alec, Leslie, Maya, Eli, Betsy, Emily, and Sarah—thanks for your love and support and for patiently understanding that Sam and I will always be the last to arrive because it takes Southern women forevah and evah to get ready.

I'd also like to thank Tedi Gibbons, my high school English and drama teacher, who was the first person to suggest I had talent that could perhaps be funneled into a career and who gave me the most valuable gift of all—confidence.

To my Gaffney gang—Leslie Potts Fulmer, Dana Phillips Pennington, April McCraw Bender, Cindy Whelchel Townsend, Nikki Hamrick Lyons, and Brad Gallman—thanks for decades of laughter, your devoted friendship, and for never letting me get too big for my britches.

I would not have the privilege of pursuing my art without the support of my loyal Pilates clients: Cindy and Craig Block, Dianne Dimascio, Garry Edelman, Jenny Graham, Alexsis Koenig, Enrique Koenig, Kassy Koenig, and Toni Spencer. Thanks to Deb Watkins at Life Long Pilates and to Maria Leone and the staff at Bodyline Pilates for their support, as well as the support of all the clients I've had the pleasure of teaching there.

Somebody's gotta be the cow's tail in this list, so last but not least, I'd like to thank my dearest—Angie Schworer, Tim Smith, Fred Pinto, Debbie Zaltman, Kisha Howard, Cristina Fortenbaugh, Lillie Kae Stevens, Amy Timmons Mahoney, Janet Ernish Dahl, Desiree Parkman, Kelli Severson Maly, Tabb Nance, and Bourbon—for always being there for me, always loving me, and always encouraging me to reach for the stars.

South Carolina native, *Julia Fowler*, is the creator of YouTube's Southern Women Channel, home of the viral video series *Sh%t Southern Women Say*. She is an actor, writer, and producer who has worked in television, film, and on Broadway. She currently resides in Venice Beach, California, and is generally irritated that it's void of proper fried okra. Visit her at www.southernwomenchannel.com.